T0323715

Cambridge Elements ≡

Elements in Pragmatics
edited by
Jonathan Culpeper
Lancaster University, UK
Michael Haugh
University of Queensland, Australia

CORPUS PRAGMATICS

Daniela Landert
Heidelberg University

Daria Dayter
Tampere University

Thomas C. Messerli
University of Basel

Miriam A. Locher
University of Basel

CAMBRIDGE
UNIVERSITY PRESS

CAMBRIDGE
UNIVERSITY PRESS

Shaftesbury Road, Cambridge CB2 8EA, United Kingdom

One Liberty Plaza, 20th Floor, New York, NY 10006, USA

477 Williamstown Road, Port Melbourne, VIC 3207, Australia

314–321, 3rd Floor, Plot 3, Splendor Forum, Jasola District Centre, New Delhi – 110025, India

103 Penang Road, #05-06/07, Visioncrest Commercial, Singapore 238467

Cambridge University Press is part of Cambridge University Press & Assessment, a department of the University of Cambridge.

We share the University's mission to contribute to society through the pursuit of education, learning and research at the highest international levels of excellence.

www.cambridge.org
Information on this title: www.cambridge.org/9781009095082
DOI: 10.1017/9781009091107

© Daniela Landert, Daria Dayter, Thomas C. Messerli and Miriam A. Locher 2023

This work is in copyright. It is subject to statutory exceptions and to the provisions of relevant licensing agreements; with the exception of the Creative Commons version the link for which is provided below, no reproduction of any part of this work may take place without the written permission of Cambridge University Press.
An online version of this work is published at doi.org/10.1017/9781009091107 under a Creative Commons Open Access license CC-BY-NC-ND 4.0 which permits re-use, distribution and reproduction in any medium for non-commercial purposes providing appropriate credit to the original work is given. You may not distribute derivative works without permission. To view a copy of this license, visit https://creativecom mons.org/licenses/by-nc-nd/4.0
All versions of this work may contain content reproduced under license from third parties.
Permission to reproduce this third-party content must be obtained from these third-parties directly.
When citing this work, please include a reference to the DOI 10.1017/9781009091107

First published 2023

A catalogue record for this publication is available from the British Library.

ISBN 978-1-009-09508-2 Paperback
ISSN 2633-6464 (online)
ISSN 2633-6456 (print)

Cambridge University Press & Assessment has no responsibility for the persistence or accuracy of URLs for external or third-party internet websites referred to in this publication and does not guarantee that any content on such websites is, or will remain, accurate or appropriate.

Corpus Pragmatics

Elements in Pragmatics

DOI: 10.1017/9781009091107
First published online: February 2023

Daniela Landert
Heidelberg University

Daria Dayter
Tampere University

Thomas C. Messerli
University of Basel

Miriam A. Locher
University of Basel

Author for correspondence: Daniela Landert,
daniela.landert@as.uni-heidelberg.de

Abstract: This Element discusses the challenges and opportunities that different types of corpora offer for the study of pragmatic phenomena. The focus lies on a hands-on approach to methods and data that provides orientation for methodological decisions. In addition, the Element identifies areas in which new methodological developments are needed in order to make new types of data accessible for pragmatic research. Linguistic corpora are currently undergoing diversification. While one trend is to move towards increasingly large corpora, another trend is to enhance corpora with more specialised and layered annotation. Both these trends offer new challenges and opportunities for the study of pragmatics. This Element provides a practical overview of state-of-the-art corpus pragmatic methods in relation to different types of corpus data, covering established methods as well as innovative approaches. This title is also available as Open Access on Cambridge Core.

Keywords: corpus-assisted pragmatics, corpus-driven pragmatics, multimodality, function-to-form mapping, comparability of corpus data

© Daniela Landert, Daria Dayter, Thomas C. Messerli and Miriam A. Locher 2023

ISBNs: 9781009095082 (PB), 9781009091107 (OC)
ISSNs: 2633-6464 (online), 2633-6456 (print)

Contents

1 Introduction

1.1 Corpora and Pragmatics

The role of corpora in pragmatic research has continually gained importance over time, and the number of published handbooks (Aijmer & Rühlemann 2014), text books (Rühlemann 2019), edited volumes (e.g. Romero-Trillo 2008; Jucker, Schreier & Hundt 2009; Suhr & Taavitsainen 2012; Taavitsainen, Jucker & Tuominen 2014) and the launch of a journal (*Corpus Pragmatics*, since 2017) demonstrate clearly that we have moved far beyond the point at which it has to be argued why corpus approaches are suitable and valuable for pragmatic studies. Corpus approaches have gained their place next to introspection, experimentation and non-corpus-based observational approaches (see Jucker, Schneider & Bublitz 2018). At the same time, there still remain many challenges for corpus approaches to pragmatic research questions. For instance, corpora still tend to be characterised by a lack of access to context, privileging of quantitative results over qualitative interpretation and focus on linguistic forms rather than their functions, all of which can hinder pragmatic studies. We believe that by taking a closer look at these challenges, we can identify new avenues in which to develop corpus pragmatics.

This introductory section presents a brief overview of the main challenges with which corpus pragmatics is faced. These challenges provide the starting point for the following sections, which deal with ways to overcome some of these challenges as well as highlighting the many benefits corpora offer for pragmatics. In doing so, we focus on the wide variety of different corpora that have become available to researchers and we explore the opportunities that each of these types of corpora provides for pragmatic studies and the research avenues that can be pursued. We adopt a wide understanding of corpora, which includes not only prototypical large and publicly released corpora, but also small, purpose-built, ad hoc collections of data. Likewise, we discuss a broad range of different approaches. What they all have in common is that they rely on digital data compilations and that they aim to identify, systematically search for and analyse linguistic patterns and their pragmatic functions with the help of computers. We place special emphasis on function-to-form approaches to corpus pragmatics. This is not to imply that form-to-function approaches are not suitable or relevant for pragmatics – they certainly are, as has been amply demonstrated. Our focus on function-to-form approaches is due to the unique challenge that they pose, given that they do not start with form-based search patterns (see Section 1.4). Since all authors of this Element work in the field of English linguistics, we will focus our discussion on English language corpora. However, the number and variety of corpora is large and continuously growing for many other languages as well, and the methods we discuss can equally be applied to corpora of other languages. Due to space restrictions, we cannot present an extensive overview of the research field, but we refer to relevant resources where interested readers can find more detailed information and overviews of the field.

1.2 Context

Pragmatic meaning is influenced by all levels of context (see Garcés-Conejos Blitvich & Sifianou 2019). On the micro level, the immediate co-text of an expression influences its interpretation. On the meso level, pragmatic meaning depends on text types, genres and thematic domains. And on the macro level, the social, cultural and historical context affects pragmatic meaning as well. As a consequence, access to contextual information is often crucial for pragmatic studies. This reliance on access to context presents what is perhaps the biggest challenge for corpus pragmatics overall. While there are some corpora that provide excellent support for accessing contextual information, many corpora – especially those that were created for studying grammar – do not sufficiently satisfy this requirement.

At the level of micro-context, access to the co-text is restricted by many corpus interfaces. Search tools mostly present results in concordance views that show the search term with a minimal co-text of a number of words to the left and right. While this word span is usually sufficient for disambiguating word meaning, it often does not provide enough information for a pragmatic analysis. Even corpus interfaces that support an expanded context view, such as the *Corpus of Contemporary American English* (*COCA*) and other corpora by the Davies corpus family, often restrict the expanded context to no more than a few lines (information on all corpora mentioned in this Element can be found in Appendix A). For some pragmatic interpretations, a few lines of context may be sufficient, but sometimes access to an entire text or conversation is crucial in order to understand how a specific utterance can be interpreted, or whether several interpretations are possible. Other popular corpus tools, like keyword analysis, collocation analysis and n-gram analysis, present results that are even more decontextualised than concordance lines.

There are at least two reasons for the tendency to restrict access to the co-text in corpora. First, copyright restrictions often keep corpus compilers from sharing full texts with users. This is the case, for instance, with many corpora that are based on films and TV series, such as the *Sydney Corpus of Television Dialogue* (*SydTV*), as well as the *SOAP Corpus*, the *Movie Corpus* and the *TV Corpus* from the Davies corpus family (Bednarek et al. 2021: 2–3). Second, most corpora that are released to the research community were not built primarily for studying pragmatics. Instead, corpus compilers often focus on grammatical and lexical characteristics. The focus of analysis influences sampling procedures and the development of corpus tools. For instance, many balanced reference corpora include text samples of a limited size, rather than entire texts. For studies of grammar, this has advantages, since it limits the possibility of the corpus being biased due to overrepresentation of individuals. For studies of pragmatics, this is true as well, but at the same time the lack of access to the larger co-text creates problems for the analysis.

With respect to the meso context, i.e. information about the genre or text type, and the thematic domain from which the corpus data was sampled, the information provided by corpora varies a great deal. Many corpora are built around one or more classifications that are relevant for studying variation across genres or text types. While some general information about this categorisation is often available, more fine-grade and more detailed information may be more difficult to access. For instance, while many balanced reference corpora include a category of news texts, distinctions into hard news dealing with political topics and soft news dealing with human interest content are less common. However, this distinction can greatly affect the use of expressions and, thus, such information can be relevant for pragmatic studies. Meso-level classifications can become especially challenging in comparisons across different corpora, when the same label is applied but the data sets are compiled according to different principles. The creation of suitable classifications that can be generalised across different corpora and types of data is often not possible, and classifications tend to vary between corpus compilers. The documentation of the sampling principles can provide valuable information on the kind of data that is included in the corpus, but sometimes this information is not easily available or not very detailed (see also Section 5).

When it comes to the macro context, the situation varies greatly across different types of corpora. Specialised corpora that include data from one specific domain are often published together with studies that present extensive discussions of the kind of data included in the corpus. In contrast, balanced reference corpora like the *British National Corpus* (*BNC*) and the *COCA* tend to assume that users are familiar with the variety that is represented. The challenge of lack of access to information about the macro context is perhaps greatest for historical corpora, where familiarity with the general socio-historical context can be taken for granted the least.

How marked the effect of research focus can be on the composition and metainformation of a corpus becomes apparent if we look at corpora that were composed with pragmatic research questions in mind. A case in point are pragmatically annotated corpora, where pragmatic information is included during the composition process (see Section 2.6). A different example can be found in certain historical corpora which were composed with a wide range of possible research aims in mind, including pragmatic questions. An example of this is the three-part *Corpus of Early English Medical Writing 1375–1800* (*CEEM*). The corpus was compiled as part of a long-running research project investigating changes in scientific thought-styles, hosted at the Research Unit for Variation, Contacts and Change in English at the University of Helsinki. The pragmatic nature of the research interest affected the corpus composition in a number of ways: the corpus includes long, 10,000 word extracts of texts rather than short samples; it comes with its own software, which provides access to passages in the context of the entire extract; it includes extensive metainformation on each text and author; and it provides direct links to additional context information, such as hyperlinks to scanned manuscript pages on *Early English Books Online* (*EEBO*) (see Tyrkkö, Hickey & Marttila 2010). All of this makes the corpus very well-suited for studies of pragmatic variables, while it can nevertheless be fruitfully used to investigate purely grammatical or lexicological research questions (e.g. Méndez-Naya & Pahta 2010).

1.3 Qualitative and Quantitative Analysis

Due to the various levels of context-dependency of pragmatic meaning, pragmatic analysis often relies quite strongly on interpretation and qualitative analysis. Researchers make judgements about the pragmatic functions of utterances by interpreting them in the context in which they are used through what is sometimes referred to as horizontal reading (Rühlemann & Aijmer 2014: 3), followed by subsequent classification. This process is time-consuming and not easily reconciled with the most prototypical uses of standard corpus tools. Most corpora are developed with the aim to support quantitative analysis and so-called vertical reading of data. They offer tools such as keyword in context (KWIC) views, normalised frequencies, keywords, collocations and n-grams. All of these tools present decontextualised or only partially contextualised views of results that help establish broader patterns across the entire corpus. When these tools are used to carry out pragmatic analysis, researchers often need to find ways of combining them with more contextualised perspectives.

In this Element, we discuss different ways in which this tension between qualitative and quantitative approaches can be resolved. The focus of Section 4 lies on corpus-assisted approaches that rely very heavily on qualitative analysis and, as a consequence, use small corpora, which still make it possible to quantify patterns in the data. In Sections 6 and 7, we focus on two areas in which we see a demand for the development of new corpus methods that take pragmatic research questions into consideration. For Section 6, these are methods that help researchers apply qualitative methods to large corpora in meaningful ways, and Section 7 turns to the analysis of multimodal data, where there is a great deal of demand for new methods that support pragmatic analysis, especially when it comes to quantifying observations.

1.4 Form-to-Function and Function-to-Form Mapping

Most pragmatic research deals with the relationship between linguistic forms and their functions. This relationship can be studied in two different ways. In form-to-function approaches, researchers study the different pragmatic functions of a given form, whereas in function-to-form approaches the aim is to identify forms with which a given function can be expressed (Jacobs & Jucker 1995: 13). Corpus pragmatics is particularly well-suited for form-to-function approaches, since corpora make it possible for researchers to search for all surface forms within the data (O'Keeffe 2018: 587). As O'Keeffe et al. (2020: 47) note, corpus linguistics overall is form-to-function oriented: apart from special cases, such as pragmatically annotated corpora, corpus searches always start with forms. Thus, it is probably no surprise that much of the early research in corpus pragmatics adopted form-to-function approaches. The study of pragmatic markers (or discourse markers) proved especially productive. An influential example of such studies is Aijmer's (2002) research monograph, which looked at a range of discourse particles, including *now*, *oh* and *ah*, and *actually* in the *London-Lund Corpus*. Other corpus-based studies on pragmatic markers have been carried out on a wide range of Present-day English (e.g. Aijmer 2008; Buysse 2012; Kirk 2015; Beeching 2016) and historical corpora (e.g. Culpeper & Kytö 2010: ch. 15; Lutzky 2012). Other examples of form-to-function approaches include the study of stance markers like *I think* (e.g. Aijmer 1997; Kärkkäinen 2003; Simon-Vandenbergen 2000) and the earlier form *methinks* (e.g. Palander-Collin 1999); the study of the pragmatic functions of *basically* (Butler 2008); the study of interjections (e.g. Norrick 2009) and the study of the planners *uh* and *um* (e.g. Tottie 2011, 2014, 2019; Tonetti Tübben & Landert 2022).

In contrast, function-to-form approaches are faced with the challenge that functions cannot be searched for automatically. This has not deterred researchers from investigating pragmatic functions in corpora, though. Speech acts in particular have been investigated with function-to-form approaches. An early example is Kohnen's (2000) study of directive speech acts in the *Lancaster–Oslo/Bergen Corpus* and the *London-Lund Corpus*. The difficulty of overcoming the lack of one-to-one correspondence between form and function is discussed very prominently in this paper. In his conclusion, Kohnen (2000: 184) states: 'It seems probable that the fundamental difficulty, the open relationship between form and function, cannot be solved ... Perhaps a corpus-based study of speech acts will have to focus on the patterns representing the most typical and common manifestations of a speech act and will not seek to cover all the possible manifestations of that speech act.' It would be overly optimistic to claim that these problems have been completely resolved in the meantime. However, research on speech acts and other function-to-form topics has made much progress (for an overview of types of approaches, see Jucker 2013). Approaches that have been developed include the search for illocutionary force indicating devices (IFIDs) (e.g. Deutschmann 2003; Jucker & Taavitsainen 2008), the search for known lexico-grammatical patterns (e.g. Adolphs 2008; Jucker et al. 2008) and the study of metacommunicative expressions (e.g. Jucker & Taavitsainen 2014; see also Haugh 2018). For research of stance expressions, the analysis of high-density passages that include clusters of known expressions has been shown to be an effective method, which may have potential for other research areas as well (Landert 2019).

Since automatic retrieval always takes place based on surface forms, even function-to-form approaches usually rely on the identification of forms in the corpus data. Exceptions to this can be found in pragmatically annotated corpora and in small-scale corpus-based approaches. In both cases, the corpus data is read and interpreted by a researcher, either as part of the compilation process (annotated corpora) or as the main focus of the analysis (small-scale corpus-based approaches). It remains an open question to what extent the identification of pragmatic functions will ever be possible without relying on predefined forms and manual evaluation.

1.5 Scalability

Scalability refers to the ease with which research methods can be applied to large sets of data. If a method is scalable, then processing a very large amount of data does not take considerably longer than processing a small amount of data. Generally speaking, quantitative methods have a much better scalability than qualitative methods. For instance, if we are interested in comparing normalised frequencies across different sets of data, the size of the data only marginally affects the duration of the calculation, as long as the number of hits can be retrieved automatically. While the automatic computation of the number of hits in the corpus increases with corpus size, it still is so fast that the duration of computation takes up a very small proportion of the overall research time. In contrast, the manual classification of pragmatic functions increases with the size of data in a linear fashion. Classifying 10,000 instances takes, roughly, 100 times as long as classifying 100 instances. In other words, manual classifications have very poor scalability.

Compared to the other challenges discussed in this section, scalability has received little attention so far. However, scalability is at the core of all of the previously discussed challenges. It is due to the poor scalability of context-dependent interpretations and the manual work involved in identifying pragmatic functions that corpora present challenges for pragmatic studies. This issue is becoming more pressing with the trend towards increasing corpus size. Larger corpora provide more data and, as a consequence, potentially more opportunities for insightful observations into pragmatic phenomena, but the large amount of work involved in qualitative analysis means that either only a small section of the data can be considered or that the focus shifts even more towards quantitative evaluations. This does not have to be the case, though. While linguists have spent a great amount of effort on developing new quantitative methods of exploring corpus data, there has been far less exploration of the ways in which we can support the qualitative analysis of data in larger corpora. As we will discuss in Section 6, it is possible, for instance, to develop semi-automated methods which rely on automated procedures to retrieve particularly relevant instances of a phenomenon for further manual analysis. Such methods help make qualitative analysis more scalable and thus open up new research perspectives for working with large corpora, even when the phenomenon under investigation relies on manual analysis.

1.6 Corpus Pragmatics and its Advantages

Despite all these challenges, corpus pragmatics is a vibrant field of research that can yield meaningful insights that complement studies on the same phenomena that were derived with different methodologies. It addresses a wide variety of research questions and makes use of a large range of corpus resources, tools and approaches. In this Element, we focus on this variety and point out those areas in which we see most potential for further developments. Throughout the Element, we highlight why it might be worth doing corpus pragmatics in the first place. Some of the advantages that corpus approaches offer can be summarised as follows:

- Pattern finding: Corpora present well-defined data sets that make it possible for researchers to identify reoccurring patterns.
- Systematicity: Corpora include samples that represent language use in a given variety or domain in a systematic way. This makes it possible to

assess the extent to which corpus data is representative of the variety or domain overall.

- Generalisation: Observations of reoccurring patterns across different sets of data make it possible to generalise findings for the language use that is represented in the corpus, provided that the corpus is compiled in a way that such generalisations are legitimate (e.g. with respect to representative sampling).
- Reproducibility: To the extent that corpus data is accessible to other researchers, and provided that methodological explanations are presented with a sufficient amount of detail, results that are based on corpora can be verified by other researchers.
- Transparency: By making use of often well-established corpus linguistic methodology, corpus pragmatics can present findings in such a way that the methodological steps that lead to them are maximally transparent.

1.7 Outline of the Element

In this Element, we do not attempt to present a comprehensive overview of corpus pragmatics. There are already various handbooks and textbooks that present excellent overviews of how different types of pragmatic phenomena can be studied with corpus data and methods (see Section 1.1). Instead, we focus on the challenges that we introduced in this section and on possible ways of addressing and overcoming them. We also want to emphasise that the term corpus can be used to refer to vastly different types of data collections: from small, manually curated compilations of project-specific datasets to huge (semi-)automatically compiled collections of electronically available documents; from data formatted and annotated for a given research objective to corpora that are compiled to ensure maximum compatibility with existing and future resources; and from purely text-based corpora to corpora including audio and video files and visual resources. This Element is structured along these distinctions, emphasising that each of these types of corpora presents unique challenges and opportunities for corpus pragmatic research.

Section 2 gives an overview of different types of corpora and how their characteristics influence pragmatic research. Each type is illustrated with examples from corpora that have been used for pragmatic studies in the past. Appendices A and B complement this section by providing lists of all corpora (Appendix A) and all corpus tools (Appendix B) mentioned in the Element. Sections 3 and 4 discuss two different ways in which purpose-built corpora can be used. In Section 3, the focus lies on corpus-driven research on project-specific data. The section discusses the manifold benefits, as well as the challenges of working with data compiled from online sources, including ethics, copyright issues and data documentation. While these issues of corpus composition are discussed in the context of corpus-driven research, many of them equally apply to corpus-based studies with self-compiled corpora. Section 4 turns to much smaller purpose-built corpora and the ways in which they can be used for corpus-assisted discourse analysis. The case study presented in the section illustrates the analytic steps needed to apply qualitative methods in such a way that quantifiable patterns can be identified in the data. Section 5 turns to the many practical challenges involved in combining different existing corpora within a single study. These challenges include, for instance, differences in data formats, annotation, metainformation and access to data, and are discussed under the keywords compatibility and comparability. While incompatibility of corpus formats can make it more difficult to work with different corpora side-by-side, the lack of comparability of data and results within or across corpora will negatively affect the reliability of results and interpretations. Section 6 deals with the issue of scalability and argues for the value of developing new scalable methods that make it possible to use large corpora even for research questions that rely on qualitative data analysis. In Section 7, we present an overview of the most recent developments in the area of multimodal corpora and discuss what is needed for pragmatic studies of such corpora. Section 8 concludes the Element with a summary of open issues and an outlook to possible future developments concerning new types of corpus resources, new methods and new research questions.

2 Corpora and their Characteristics: Challenges and Opportunities for Pragmatic Research

2.1 Introduction

In this Element, we adopt a broad perspective on corpus pragmatics and corpora. We present an overview of the many different ways in which corpora can be used for pragmatic research. In order to do so, it is necessary to point out the wide variety of linguistic corpora that exist today, which is the topic of this section. Our aim is not to present a comprehensive list of all corpora – not only would this be an impossible task but the list would be outdated very quickly – but rather to introduce distinctions between types of corpora as discussed in the literature, many of which will be relevant for the remaining sections in the Element.

In what follows, we decided to introduce examples of what the research community has coined at various times as types of corpora of interest to pragmatics: balanced reference corpora, topic- and domain-specific corpora, spoken corpora, multimodal corpora, pragmatically annotated corpora, learner corpora, parallel multilingual corpora, corpora including unsystematic large text collections and purpose-built self-compiled corpora. However, the distinctions between these categories are in fact fuzzy and they are not mutually exclusive. In other words, corpora can belong to more than one group. For instance, there are balanced reference corpora that include multimodal spoken data in the form of audio recordings (e.g. *BNC2014*), topic-specific large text collections (e.g. *News on the Web*) and topic-specific learner corpora (e.g. the *Giessen–Long Beach Chaplin Corpus*). And, of course, there are other distinctions that could be added to the list, such as diachronic corpora and corpora of child language acquisition (e.g. Child Language Data Exchange System (*CHILDES*)). For a rough and incomplete overview meant to highlight this fuzzy nature of the categories, see Table 1. As a consequence, rather than suggesting a fixed taxonymy-type list, we selected the distinctions to draw attention to those opportunities and challenges of corpus pragmatics where we see most potential for research developments at the moment.

In Section 2.2, we start our discussion with a group of corpora that describes some of the oldest and still very common corpora, namely balanced reference corpora. Their counterpoint are topic-specific corpora, discussed in Section 2.3. The next two sections deal with modality. In Section 2.4, we describe corpora that are based on spoken language and in Section 2.5, we discuss the multimodal representation of data in corpora. Section 2.6 focuses on corpora that include pragmatic annotation. The following two sections deal with what language is represented in a corpus. Corpora on learner English are discussed in Section 2.7, and Section 2.8 introduces parallel multilingual corpora. The final two sections deal with size and data selection. Corpora that are based on unsystematic large text collections are discussed in Section 2.9, and Section 2.10 starts the discussion of purpose-built self-compiled corpora, which will be continued in Sections 3 and 4. Each distinction is introduced briefly and a few examples of relevant corpora are mentioned. We also present some advantages and limitations of such corpora for pragmatic research and provide a few examples of pragmatic studies that have been carried out in the past.

The corpus landscape is changing quickly. For up-to-date information of existing corpora and their accessibility, electronic sources are far more suitable than printed publications. There is not a uniform point of access for all existing linguistic corpus resources, although various attempts at establishing repositories of corpus data and/or information about corpora have been made. Corpora can be found, for instance, in research infrastructures like the *Common Language Resources and Technology Infrastructure* (*CLARIN*), online repositories like the *Oxford Text Archive* (*OTA*) and corpus managers like *Sketch Engine*.

Table 1 Overview of a selection of corpora and the corpus categories they simultaneously belong to, ordered alphabetically according to the name of the corpus

Corpus categories→ Name of corpus↓	balanced reference corpus	topic- and domain-specific corpora	spoken corpora	multimodal corpora	pragmatically annotated corpora	learner corpora	unsystematic large text collections
BNC 1994	x		(x)	(audio)			
CHILDES		x	x	audio/video			
CLMET3.0		x					x
EEBO		x					x
Giessen–Long Beach Chaplin Corpus		x	x	audio		x	
ICE	x		(x)				
LINDSEI			x			x	
Longman Corpus of Spoken and Written English	x	x	(x)				
News on the Web		x					x
NMMC		x	x	audio/video			
SBC			x	audio	x		
SPICE-Ireland Corpus			x		x		
VOICE			x	(audio)			

All abbreviations of corpora mentioned in Table 1 can be found in the discussion in this section.

x: applies

(x): transcripts only

A valuable database of information about English language corpora is the *Corpus Resource Database* (*CoRD*), which includes a corpus finder tool that filters corpora according to language period, word count, type of data and annotation, and availability.

2.2 Balanced Reference Corpora

Balanced reference corpora are corpora that include text samples from a variety of different contexts in order to provide an overall representation of a given language variety. One of the most frequently used reference corpora is the *BNC*. It includes different types of spoken and written language samples from British English. While the original corpus, the *BNC1994*, included data from the 1990s, the recently released *BNC2014* adds data from around 2014, thus providing opportunities for investigations into recent language change. Other examples are *COCA* and the *International Corpus of English* (*ICE*). The latter consists of an entire collection of corpora that represent English varieties from around the world. Another group of reference corpora are the corpora used as a basis for compiling dictionaries and grammars, such as the *Longman Corpus of Spoken and Written English*. Important diachronic reference corpora of English are the *Helsinki Corpus of English Texts* (*HC*) and the *ARCHER* corpus, and, for American English, the *Corpus of Historical American English* (*COHA*).

Advantages: Balanced reference corpora provide a general-purpose perspective on a language variety and are particularly well-suited for investigating general characteristics of a language variety. They are also very suitable for studying register variation, e.g. the variation of language phenomena across different text types and genres.

Limitations: Balanced reference corpora are usually compiled for facilitating the study of lexico-grammatical characteristics. They usually only support form-based queries and they often present decontextualised views of the data with limited access to context.

Examples of previous studies: Many form-to-function studies have been based on balanced reference corpora, e.g. the study of discourse markers (e.g. Aijmer 2002, 2008) and planners (Tottie 2011). Apologies have been studied in the *BNC* (Deutschmann 2003) and the *COHA* (Jucker 2018).

2.3 Topic- and Domain-Specific Corpora

Corpora can be compiled for any given topic or domain. Examples of recently released corpora include *SydTV*, based on transcripts of language used in television series; the *Brexit Corpus*, a 100-million-word collection of online texts relating to the UK referendum on Brexit; and the *Corpus of Historical English Law Reports 1535–1999 (CHELAR)*. They are often compiled for a specific research project and, thus, their composition, annotation and suitability for pragmatic studies varies a great deal. While a single corpus only provides insight into one domain, different corpora can sometimes be combined to gain a broader perspective (see Section 5).

Advantages: Those topic- and domain-specific corpora that were compiled with pragmatic research questions in mind often offer annotation and contextual information that make them extremely suitable for pragmatic studies.

Limitations: Given that many domain-specific corpora were compiled for a specific research project, it can be challenging for other researchers to use these corpora for different projects. The composition, markup and metainformation may be geared towards some research questions rather than others. Consulting corpus documentations and learning about the corpus data is perhaps even more important than for other corpora. In some cases, it can be difficult to gain access to documentation or the information provided may be insufficient. However, some domain-specific corpora are also among the corpora with the most detailed amount of background information.

Examples of previous studies: There are many different kinds of examples that could be quoted here. Lutzky and Kehoe's (2017a, 2017b) studies of apologies in the *Birmingham Blog Corpus (BBC)* are an example of research based on contemporary data. Examples of studies on historical corpora are Traugott's (2015) study of interjections in the *Old Bailey Corpus (OBC)*, Culpeper and Kytö's (2010) study of pragmatic noise in the *Corpus of English Dialogues 1560–1760 (CED)*, and various studies on the development of scientific thought-styles that are based on the *Corpus of Early English Medical Writing (CEEM)* (e.g. Gray, Biber & Hiltunen 2011; Taavitsainen 2001, 2002, 2009; Whitt 2016).

2.4 Spoken Corpora

Early corpora that were based on spoken language data, such as the original *London-Lund Corpus (LLC)* often included only written transcriptions. In recent years, it has become more and more common to provide access to audio recordings, which are often aligned with the written corpus data, which makes them multimodal corpora (see Section 2.5 and Section 7). Examples are the spoken section of the original *British National Corpus (BNC1994)*, for which recordings have recently been made accessible, as well as the recently released new corpus component *BNC2014* and the soon-to-be released *London–Lund Corpus 2 (LLC2)*. The *Santa Barbara Corpus of American English (SBC)* is another important resource for the study of spoken language, consisting of sixty recordings and corresponding transcriptions. More specialised spoken corpora include the *Cambridge and Nottingham Business English Corpus* (*CANBEC*), *British Academic Spoken English Corpus* (*BASE*) and the *Vienna-Oxford International Corpus of English* (*VOICE*), which includes spoken language data from speakers of English as a lingua franca. In addition to differences in the availability of audio recordings, the corpora vary greatly with respect to the degree of detail and the amount of prosodic information that is included in the transcriptions.

Advantages: In addition to presenting data from one important mode of language realisation, spoken language corpora that provide access to audio recordings can give insight into how paraverbal features like loudness, stress, speech rhythm and other prosodic features affect pragmatic functions, an aspect that has not been explored in great detail so far (see also Section 2.5).

Limitations: The integration of written transcriptions and audio recordings poses challenges. The new *BNC* interface has made great progress in this respect, even making it possible to search for phonological phenomena. Still, search queries usually rely on written transcriptions and the transcription conventions vary a great deal across different corpora.

Examples of previous studies: Adolphs & Carter (2013) present a very detailed discussion of spoken corpus linguistics, which includes studies on pragmatic aspects such as response tokens.

2.5 Multimodal Corpora

Multimodal corpora are corpora which, in addition to text, also include data in different modalities. For instance, this can take the form of audio recordings of spoken language or visual information in the form of still images or videos. There are many different ways in which data in different modalities is presented. The most basic form can be found in corpora that include separate files with the different modalities, such as the *SBC*. The *SBC* consists of a collection of discourse analytic transcriptions of spoken language recordings, and the recordings are provided as separate audio files. At the opposite end of the scale we can find corpus infrastructures that include multilayered annotation of data aligned across different modalities. An example of this latter type is the *Nottingham Multimodal Corpus* (*NMMC*), which includes video recordings, transcriptions of the spoken language and the annotation of non-verbal communication like gestures.

Advantages: Multimodal spoken corpora make it possible for researchers to study verbal, paraverbal and non-verbal features of language in combination.

In written language, the combination of text with images, videos, layout and typographic elements can be studied. Thus, multimodal corpora open up new avenues of pragmatic research.

Limitations: By far the biggest limitation of multimodal corpora is that their compilation is very time-consuming and, as a consequence, they tend to be rather small. Corpora that include layers of annotation for non-textual information, such as gestures or eye-gaze, face the same challenges as transcriptions of spoken language, namely that the transcription of such information involves a considerable deal of qualitative interpretation.

Examples of previous studies: We discuss different examples of studies based on multimodal corpora in Section 7.

2.6 Pragmatically Annotated Corpora

Some corpora include annotation that is relevant for pragmatic analysis (for an overview, see O'Keeffe 2018: 599–605). In some cases, corpus annotations can inform pragmatic analysis, whereas in others, it is pragmatic information that is annotated. For instance, the *Sociopragmatic Corpus* (*SPC*) is a subsection of the *CED*, in which speaker information such as gender, social status, role and age group is annotated on the level of each utterance. This makes it possible to study, for instance, how the role relationship between interlocutors affects the realisation of pragmatic functions. An example of annotation of pragmatic information can be found in the *SPICE-Ireland Corpus*, a subsection of the spoken component of the *ICE-Ireland* corpus that is annotated for pragmatic and prosodic information. The annotation includes information about the speech-act function of utterances, discourse markers and quotatives.

Advantages: Depending on the kind of annotation, annotated corpora make it possible for researchers to search for pragmatic functions or to restrict their queries to factors that are relevant for pragmatic analysis.

Limitations: Since annotation is time-consuming, these corpora tend to be small. Attempts at automatising the process have been made (see Weisser 2014 on the automatic annotation of speech acts), but it is doubtful whether the process of manual classification will ever be fully replaced and, thus, the time needed to add annotations to a corpus will likely continue to pose limits to the size of annotated corpora. Moreover, studies are restricted to the kinds of information that have been annotated in the corpus, and given that the annotation of pragmatic information already involves a great deal of interpretation, the corpus compiler's assessment of the data influences the results.

Examples of previous studies: Kirk's (2015) study of the pragmatic markers *kind of* and *sort of* is based on the *SPICE-Ireland Corpus*. The *Sociopragmatic Corpus* has been used for a range of studies on pragmatic features in Early Modern English, including Archer's (2005) studies of questions and answers, Culpeper and Archer's (2008) study of requests and Lutzky's (2012) study of discourse markers.

2.7 Learner Corpora

Learner corpora include language produced by non-native speakers of a language. Such corpora usually provide information on the level of proficiency and/or the amount of instruction of the speakers or writers that contribute data. Examples of learner corpora are the *International Corpus of Learner English* (*ICLE*), based on essays from learners from a large number of different language backgrounds, and the *Louvain International Database of Spoken English Interlanguage* (*LINDSEI*), the spoken counterpart to *ICLE*.

Advantages: Learner corpora make it possible to study pragmatic aspects of L2 language learning. They can also provide new perspectives for language teaching.

Limitations: The data in learner corpora is often derived from task-based language production. While written learner corpora may include essays that were produced in the ordinary course of the teaching process, spoken corpora often include task-based interaction that took place for the purpose of corpus composition, and that sometimes also includes language produced by interviewers involved in corpus composition. This distinguishes learner corpora from most other kinds of corpora, which tend to include language that was produced without elicitation for research purposes.

Examples of previous studies: Examples of corpus studies of pragmatic features in learner corpora include the study of hesitation markers (Gilquin 2008) and discourse markers (Buysse 2012, 2017, 2020) based on the *LINDSEI* corpus. Another example is Huschová's (2021) study of the pragmatic functions of *can* and *could* in speech acts in the *Corpus of Czech Students' Spoken English*.

2.8 Parallel Multilingual Corpora

The term 'parallel corpus' refers to a corpus of specific design, which includes related subcorpora aligned in respect to one another according to certain criteria (these might be structural, e.g. sentence or timestamp alignment, or semantic, e.g. translation unit alignment). A multilingual parallel corpus contains source texts, or transcripts, in one language, and their translation(s) into other language(s).

The parallel aligned design makes it possible to locate an excerpt in the source text and its corresponding translation using a single query. Various parallel corpora are available to date (see Examples of previous studies). For researchers interested in compiling their own parallel multilingual corpus, SketchEngine offers a corpus infrastructure that supports this.

Advantages: Parallel corpora enabled a qualitatively new step in the studies of translation and cross-linguistic analysis, finally making it possible to test empirically the assumptions about translation universals, improve machine translation and provide translators with a more reliable, up-to-date and usage-based alternative to a conventional dictionary.

Limitations: Parallel corpora are notoriously difficult to compile since they require an additional step of aligning the subcorpora. This has prompted calls to reuse existing parallel corpora rather than invest in the creation of new purpose-built ones (Doval & Sánchez Nieto 2019). In addition, professional translators in large organisations often rely on shared translation memories such as DGT-TM, i.e. organisation-specific databases that store sentences, paragraphs or segments of text that have been translated before. This makes the resulting translation corpora uninteresting for research in contrastive linguistics (Cartoni et al. 2013).

Examples of previous studies: The key resources of this type, such as the *EUROPARL* (the proceedings from the European Union in twenty-one languages, see Koehn 2005) or *OPUS* (subtitles and localisation resources covering 200 language variants, see Tiedemann 2012), generated hundreds of studies. They range from classic issues of translation studies, e.g. testing the explicitation hypothesis (Zufferey & Cartoni 2014), to research questions in contrastive linguistics, e.g. studying how impersonalisation is expressed in English versus German (Gast 2015).

2.9 Unsystematic Large Text Collections

There are a number of interfaces that make it possible for researchers to search collections of often unannotated electronic documents that were not systematically selected to build a linguistic corpus. A prominent example is the *Google Ngram Viewer*, which can be used to compare the frequencies of word sequences in printed (and electronically available) sources since 1500. Similarly, *EEBO* provides a search interface for almost 150,000 titles of historical printed books from 1475 to 1640. With *EEBO*, researchers have the option of searching for some amount of metainformation on the books, as well as of viewing images of page scans of the book. However, there is only limited access to the full text of *EEBO* and more advanced corpus operations – e.g. search for collocations and keywords – cannot be carried out. Similarly to *EEBO*, the *Corpus of Late Modern English Texts* (*CLMET 3.0*) provides access to the full books published by British authors between 1710 and 1920.

Advantages: The main advantage of such search interfaces is that they often provide access to a massive amount of data. This is especially valuable for studying less frequent linguistic phenomena, for which large corpora are needed to find a sufficient number of attestations. In addition, large text collections can provide some insight into overall diachronic developments, especially when different expressions are compared to each other. Finally, large amounts of data are ideal for the training of machine learning language models, which can be used for the computational analysis of linguistic features, including pragmatic ones.

Limitations: Unsystematic text collections do not have the same degree of reliability as smaller, manually compiled corpora. Documents can be misclassified, leading to wrong results, and automatic text recognition, which is often used in preparing the data, can misrepresent the content of documents. These problems can be reduced by editing the data, but due to the data size, this process is often time-consuming. In addition, contextualisation is often a problem. For instance, the *Google Ngram Viewer* only provides frequencies of word sequences, but there is no option of viewing instances of the sequence in context. These limitations mean that such data sources can usually only provide one piece of information, which has to be complemented with additional evidence through triangulation of methods.

Examples of previous studies: The *Google Ngram Viewer* has been used in various studies of metacommunicative expressions, such as in Jucker and Kopaczyk's (2017) account of historical (im)politeness. Likewise, Jucker (2020) presents results from *CLMET*, in addition to the *Google Ngram Viewer*, in tracing politeness expressions across time.

2.10 Purpose-Built Self-Compiled Corpora

Many corpus-based studies of pragmatics are based on corpora that are purpose-built for the study in question. Depending on the project for which they are created, such self-compiled corpora can vary greatly in size, composition and metainformation that is included. They can take the form of small, carefully selected and richly annotated collections of data as well as vast compilations of documents that are electronically available. Likewise, they may or may not be made accessible to other researchers (see also Limitations).

Self-compiled corpora can be processed with generic corpus software, which includes freeware such as *AntConc*, *TXM* and the tools offered by the *IMS Open Corpus Workbench* (*CWB*), as well as paid solutions like *WordSmith Tools* or *Sketch Engine*. For smaller projects and qualitatively oriented research questions, tools for qualitative data analysis can be used, such as *MAXQDA, NVivo* and *ATLAS.ti*. For researchers comfortable with using programming languages, additional tools are available, such as *Python's Natural Language Toolkit* (*NLTK*) and *spaCy*, or *R*'s *quanteda* and *koRpus*. For many purposes, a good text editor and pattern-matching with regular expressions can be sufficient to help researchers process text-based data. For more advanced analysis, XML-based corpora can be annotated and searched with XPath or CSS Queries, for instance using the *Oxygen XML Editor*. *CWB* corpora can be hosted on a server and made accessible via a graphic user interface (*CQPweb*).

Advantages: Purpose-built corpora present exactly the kind of data that is needed to answer a given research question. In addition, researchers who compile their own corpora tend to be extremely familiar with the data that is included, which is of great advantage for interpretation.

Limitations: The biggest drawback of self-compiled corpora is probably the amount of work needed for compiling them. This is one of the arguments in favour of making corpora accessible to other researchers, so that they can benefit from the work as well. Another argument is transparency. Only by providing data access to other researchers can results be verified independently. The FAIR Principles (www.go-fair.org/fair-principles/) discuss the relevant considerations behind this. Moreover, researchers need to deal not only with technical issues, such as suitable data repositories, standards of file formats and annotation, but also with a large range of ethical and legal questions concerning data collection and sharing (see Section 3.3). The latter concerns are, of course, also an issue for the corpus compilers of other corpus types but no longer for the users of the finished corpora, who rely on ethics and copyright having been taken care of by the compilers.

Examples of previous studies: We discuss different examples of studies using purpose-built self-compiled corpora in Sections 3 and 4.

2.11 Conclusion

The outline of corpus categories presented in this section makes it clear that corpora come in all kinds of sizes, forms and structures, and with a wide variety of different kinds of contents. As a consequence, corpus pragmatics is far from a homogenous field of research. Methods that are well-suited for searching text in balanced sampler corpora cannot be applied directly to the analysis of gestures in multimodal corpora, and the skills needed by researchers for compiling and annotating their own handcrafted datasets will differ vastly from the skills needed to work with interfaces to unsystematic large text collections. Thus, any discussion of corpus pragmatic methods needs to first establish what kind of corpus data is involved in a given study. In the remainder of this Element, we take a closer look at some types of corpora and the kinds of challenges and opportunities they present for research.

3 Corpus-Driven Approaches with Self-Compiled Corpora

3.1 Introduction

The distinction between corpus-based and corpus-driven approaches to linguistics was introduced by Tognini-Bonelli (2001), who discussed the underlying assumptions behind corpus work with language data. She posited that while corpus-based studies use a systematically collected dataset – a corpus – in order to test or explore a pre-existing hypothesis, corpus-driven studies claim that the corpus itself is the sole source of hypothesis about language. A corpus-driven approach to pragmatics, therefore, treats a corpus as more than a repository of examples or a reference for a bottom-up development of evolving taxonomies (as with the methods described in Section 4 of this Element).

While corpora are often created with the aim to allow analyses relatively free from preconceived notions about language, it is important to note that corpus building is itself an analytical step and that no corpus is theory-free. This is especially true for corpus-driven pragmatics, since pragmatic meaning is necessarily more interpretative than, say, lexicogrammar. In order to remove researchers' bias as far as possible, corpus-driven approaches rely on automatic annotation of pragmatic phenomena. As such, corpus-driven research requires relatively large corpora and sophisticated automatic annotation. Pragmatic annotation layers may include classic pragmatic units (speech acts, deixis) and units on the interface between pragmatics and semantics (such as contextualisation cues or positive versus negative polarity). Some scholars draw on grammatical annotation for corpus pragmatics as well, arguing that the creation of communicative meaning involves all levels of language (for instance, Rühlemann & Clancy 2018, who study indicative and subjunctive verb forms as an expression of deixis).

The work on (semi)automatic speech-act annotation of English language corpora includes the *Speech Act Annotated Corpus* project (*SPAAC*, University of Lancaster, Leech & Weisser 2003) and the implementations of the *Dialogue Annotation & Research Tool* (*DART*, Weisser 2010, 2015). Of course, some speech acts lend themselves better to automatic annotation than others. For example, congratulations are strongly associated with predictable surface forms such as 'congratulations', 'happy birthday', 'merry Christmas' – the so-called IFIDs. The bulk of corpus pragmatic research within the corpus-driven approach has been done on speech acts with a stable list of IFIDs, for example, apologies (Lutzky & Kehoe 2017a; Jucker 2018). Some ambitious attempts in natural language processing aimed to include more contextual factors when training an algorithm to recognise speech acts that do not include IFIDs – for example, flirting (see Ranganath et al. 2009).

In this section of the Element, we zero in on a special case of corpus-driven pragmatics: when researchers rely on fully automatic extraction of linguistic features but steer their interest through the process of corpus compilation. Much of automatic corpus analysis relies on the comparison of subcorpora (for example, keyword analysis, contrasting lists of n-grams or ranking collocates of an item). This means that through corpus design, researchers can manifest their interest in specific variables, while keeping the study of those variables entirely corpus-driven. For example, compiling a corpus of book reviews with different reader ratings enables the researcher to analyse how polarity and evaluation differ depending on whether a book is liked (Rebora et al. 2021: ii240–1).

In this section, we will discuss the process of creating such a corpus, and the benefits and challenges of this type of corpus pragmatic research, based on the example of the r/changemyview study of persuasion. The challenges and choices of the corpus creation process that are discussed in this section are not unique to corpus-driven pragmatic research and can be usefully applied in other research contexts, including those described in Section 4. The present corpus was created by downloading posts and replies from the popular online forum website Reddit (www.reddit.com/) (See Dayter & Messerli 2022). Reddit is a platform subdivided into thousands of thematic forum communities, many of which lend themselves well to the study of specific pragmatic phenomena. Below, we discuss a purpose-built corpus of the forum threads from the r/changemyview (*CMV*) subreddit (www.reddit.com/r/changemyview/), a community devoted to persuasive practices.

3.2 Case study: Persuasion in a Corpus of Reddit Posts

3.2.1 Designing a Corpus for the Study of Persuasion

Persuasive discourse has been defined in linguistic research as all linguistic behaviour that attempts to either change the thinking or behaviour of an audience, or to strengthen its beliefs, should the audience already agree (Virtanen & Halmari 2005).

Since the judgement of whether a stretch of discourse is persuasive or not (i.e. has changed or strengthened the readers' views) depends on the speaker's or writer's intent, the decision is ultimately interpretative and would have to be realised through the process of manual annotation.

However, through the careful choice of data and corpus design, researchers can enable a corpus-driven pragmatic study. The first step in this process is to find a dataset that contains persuasive discourse, recognised as such through both interaction-internal and interaction-external orientation. A good example of data of this kind can be found on the subreddit r/changemyview. Not only does the subreddit self-identify as a community dedicated to changing users' views, comments posted on it also include several language-external indicators of popularity and persuasiveness. One of these indicators, called karma, is Reddit's equivalent to upvotes and likes on other platforms and social networks and points to the uptake of individual posts by other members of the community. Collaboratively, the community thus signals their approval by adding to the post's and poster's karma. In addition, and more importantly for the persuasion-oriented researcher, threads of comments on *CMV* award a great deal of inter-actional power to original posters (henceforward OP). OPs first post a statement with an invitation for others to change their, the OP's, view. When comments are posted, OPs then decide which of them succeeded in persuading them and reward such convincing posts with a delta (Δ), which signals to others that the OP found the arguments in the awarded post persuasive. Consequently, the researcher who collects a corpus of *CMV* data and includes delta awards as metadata, can structure their data so that successfully persuasive comments (delta-awarded comments, DACs) and unsuccessful attempts at persuasion (non-DACs) can be contrasted. Without the limitations of automatic annotation of pragmatic features, or the etic judgement of one or several trained coders, it is thus possible to create a large corpus of attempts at persuasion and subcorpora of more and less persuasive comments (Dayter & Messerli 2022).

3.2.2 Building a Corpus: Ethics and Copyright

The first concern of any empirical project is the availability and researchability of data, which means that researchers must inevitably ask themselves first whether the data they want to study can be acquired in a manner that is both ethically sound and in agreement with existing copyright laws. While smaller qualitative studies primarily establish this by getting the explicit consent of the rights holders to the data they use (typically the authors themselves), research based on larger corpora cannot follow the same pattern, since it is not feasible to ask, say, hundreds of thousands of *CMV* users for permission to use their data.

This has been recognised in recent times also by new legislation, e.g. in Germany and Switzerland, where some of us work, which specifically allows big data research without consent for scientific purposes. Following these laws is the first step in ensuring sound research, but it does not exempt researchers from carefully assessing the ethical ramifications of their research for the people whose work they are scrutinising. Just like in the case of studies based on consent, researchers need to also ask themselves whether their studies will be beneficial or could potentially be harmful for authors represented in the corpus as well as for society at large. A useful guide for interpreting the existing ethics guidelines with respect to corpus linguistic approaches can be found, for example, in Koene and Adolphs (2015), focusing on internet data, or the AoIR Internet Research Ethics 3.0 (franzke et al. 2020), addressing specifically the problem of informed consent in big data analyses.

In the example we choose here, the researchers established that the population chosen for research is not vulnerable and the textual data does not concern issues that might cause potential harm if disclosed in publication. Moreover, the subreddit r/changemyview encourages academic research and has a page dedicated to academic papers using *CMV* data. Therefore, there is no potential harm to social media users, or potential ethical problems associated with the project.

In addition to ethics concerning those whose work is included in the corpus, there are further ethical concerns and responsibilities towards the scientific community. In this sense, ethical research always attempts to be optimally transparent and to facilitate reproducibility of its result. It is worth pointing out, however, that ethical concerns for the research community and for the researched population are often at odds. Researchers find themselves confronted with the uncomfortable choice of increasing the potential for harmful outcomes for the communities they research or reducing the transparency of research, with the latter typically considered the lesser evil. Thus, the consensus in research ethics is that social media posts should not be redistributed as datasets, since this denies agency to individuals who have subsequently deleted their posts and may be entirely unaware that their data are circulating in third-party datasets shared among researchers (see Proferes et al. 2021). This stance is fixed both in the Twitter's Terms of Service and, more generally, in European GDPR's stipulation on the right to be forgotten. The compromise to satisfy the demand on reproducibility is to create 'dehydrated datasets', i.e. lists of unique post IDs instead of files with full textual data and metadata.

3.2.3 Building a Corpus: Technical Challenges

A corpus in the sense we are using it here is typically an operational representation of the linguistic practices of a community. In our example, the researchers considered the subreddit *CMV* as a speech community whose interactions, while being perhaps similar to others on Reddit, in social media and elsewhere, can reasonably be modelled in a research corpus for internal as well as contrastive studies. Since the corpus is thus in a particular relationship to that which it models, i.e. to the utterances that were and are accessible on r/changemymiew, researchers are faced with decisions about how to represent the population in the corpus. Choices include such aspects as:

– The amount of data – how many posts should be included in the corpus?
– Which texts, if any, should be excluded from the corpus – e.g. duplicates
– The representation of each text, including typography, aesthetic presentation, and linguistic, paralinguistic, and non-linguistic context (see Section 7 for considerations concerning multimodality)
– The inclusion of internal and external metadata – e.g. delta, the time of posting or information about the individual posters
– The hierarchy of and relationship between texts in the corpus
– Additional annotations that should be added by the researchers to facilitate their research

In the case of the *CMV* corpus, the researchers chose to collect all posts that had ever been posted to r/changemyview, which means that it would include all posts between May 2013 and the time of data collection, May 2020. When it comes to excluding texts, corpus-building choices reflected what is and is not considered to be a part of *CMV* communication: in some cases, posts marked as deleted can still be accessed through the pushshift.io Reddit API that was used to collect the data, as are those that are marked as being in breach of the subreddit's rules. Both these types of posts were excluded from the final corpus. In addition, the cut-off date points to a problem concerning the fixity of the text (Jucker 2004). While the raw data of social media in particular may grow indefinitely (submissions to r/changemyview written before 2020 may still receive comments years later), the static representation in the corpus is often fixed at the time of collection, thus forcing dynamically evolving discourse into a rigid snapshot. Corpora such as Davies' *NOW* (*News on the Web*) corpus may instead be updated at regular intervals and thus be conceptually dynamic. Since published research is largely static at the time of rewriting, a more dynamic approach creates issues in terms of reproducibility, and in the inevitable choice between the two strategies, the researchers building the *CMV* corpus thus chose stability of results over representation of dynamic data.

In terms of the representation of the texts, the *CMV* corpus only included verbatim the roughly six million texts themselves, but not their visual organisation into threads, no audiovisual materials users may have posted alongside their texts (of which there are very few if any), and no typographic and other aspects of the graphic appearance on Reddit. The corpus includes metadata that is also visible on r/changemyview, like the time of posting, the delta status of posts – were they awarded a delta or not? – and a unique user for each comment. However, for ethical reasons all user names were anonymised. The relationship between texts was also represented as textual metadata, with hierarchies flattened into annotations as to what threads comments belong to and what posts or comments they respond to. Finally, regarding additional annotations, the corpus was lemmatised and tagged for parts of speech.

While the *CMV* corpus exists in an initial form, encoded in the *CWB* (see Evert & Hardie 2011) and accessible locally through command line tools as well as using the *R* package *polmineR* (Blaette 2020), it is important to point out that individual studies will typically use corpora in particular ways, which often amount to actually or virtually creating new corpora or subcorpora and thus new representations of aspects of communication in the original population. In the *CMV* project, an initial focus was a contrastive study of linguistic differences between more and less successfully persuasive posts (see Section 3.2.4). Accordingly, the corpus was subsampled into two subcorpora based on the delta-marker: a 14.5 million word delta subcorpus (54,000 texts) was compared to a 133.7 million word non-delta corpus (500,000 texts). In this case, the delta subcorpus contains all comments available in the corpus and thus on r/changemyview (in May 2020), whereas the non-delta segment contains a sizeable sample of the population. This sampling of the non-delta subcorpus included the conscious choice to increase the similarities to the delta subcorpus, which meant that very short and very long texts were included until an almost identical average word length was achieved (266–7 words per comment).

3.2.4 Analysis of Formality and Persuasion

Based on the corpus design we illustrated above, the researchers in the *CMV* project conducted two studies targeting register differences in the *CMV* corpus. The detailed results of the first study are published in Dayter and Messerli (2022), with the second study forthcoming. Rather than reiterating these results here in full, we will offer a brief summary and use Section 3.3 primarily to highlight the insights the studies offer for corpus-driven research more broadly.

Using a comparative subcorpus design, we have investigated the linguistic differences between delta and non-delta comments along two dimensions: formality–informality and overt expression of persuasion. To operationalise the linguistic exploration of the delta/non-delta distinction inherent in the population and the corpus, procedures established and documented in the existing literature were used. The first study identified twelve quantifiable linguistic markers (for example, frequency of WH questions and of nominalisations) that are associated either with high-formality or low-formality language. The second study drew on Biber's (1988) variationist analysis, which has proposed and empirically validated seven linguistic features associated with the overt persuasion dimension of variation (such as frequency of infinitive, prediction modals or suasive verbs).

After a statistical analysis (the chosen method here was the Mann–Whitney *U* test, a test that can be used to compare data that is not normally distributed), we arrived at the conclusion that there are no significant differences of high or medium effect between the delta and non-delta posts. This was true both for the formality and for the overt persuasiveness dimensions. The studies fell squarely into the category of negative results – a situation when the anticipated hypothesis is not borne out by the corpus data.

Taken in isolation, the results of this corpus-driven study did not contribute in a significant way to our understanding of persuasive language on *CMV*. However, it is exactly in this context that the benefits of combining corpus-driven methods with a closer inspection of the language data become apparent. To triangulate the quantitative findings, we designed our study to also include manual analysis of the concordances of two category-bound actions: *to persuade* and *to change someone's view*, as well as a study of the highest-frequency n-grams. This closer look at community discourses revealed an explicit orientation towards how, in the opinion of community members, a hypothetical 'good user' or 'good persuader' should write. The users frequently referred to the binary distinction between a personal opinion that cannot be changed by facts and evidence (an undesirable stance) versus a malleable view that can be disproven in an objective manner (desirable stance). The two example below illustrate this community norm:

(3.1) We can't really change your view of a personal opinion. If you don't enjoy ET then you don't enjoy ET.

(3.2) First, you can change your view multiple times, and you claimed secular buddhismis the most common, and I disproved that with numbers.

As Example 3.2 shows, 'change your view' is often understood as 'provide evidence that your view is incorrect'. The members of the *CMV* community recognise formal register as the appropriate linguistic resource to draw on in evidence-oriented discourse. Taken together, the corpus and the qualitative analytical findings confirmed that r/changemyview has an established linguistic community norm: all users write in a formal, overtly persuasive style, perhaps reflecting the community's affinity for academic-like argumentation.

3.3 Conclusion

Corpus-driven approaches to pragmatics aim to be as unbiased by pre-existing assumptions about the dataset as possible. This stance is very useful when working with pragmatic categories that can boast robust form-to-function correlation, for example deixis or discourse markers. However, adding an interpretative component in an analysis of higher-level 'strategies' or 'moves' inevitably requires a departure from an approach to data completely uninformed by any pre-existing theory. In this section, we demonstrated how a compromise may be achieved through careful preliminary corpus design, which is then used as the sole source of hypothesis about language in line with the corpus-driven pragmatics setup. Despite the overall success of the approach, some interesting observations resulting from the study could only be put in sufficient context with help of a qualitative close-up look. The next section of the Element, Section 4, will continue down this avenue of research to describe the benefits and limitations of corpus-based and corpus-assisted approaches to pragmatics.

4 Corpus-Assisted Approaches with Self-Compiled Corpora

4.1 Introduction: Corpora in Discourse Analysis

Corpus pragmatics is an important field of research that enables linguists to analyse public discourses about societal issues, such as gender politics and gender relations (Lutzky & Lawson 2019), voting behaviour (Ifukor 2010), right-wing activism and misogyny (Krendel et al. 2022), terrorism (Harrison et al. 2008) or the anti-vaccination movement (Quo VaDis Project 2022). However, traditional corpus-driven methods (such as the ones described in Section 3 of this Element) may lack the human analyst's judgement, which is highly important for understanding discourse. The gap between an automatic analysis of corpora of moderate to large scale and a close reading of each example by a human can be bridged by corpus-assisted approaches to pragmatics and discourse analysis.

More qualitatively oriented researchers make use of a number of corpus-assisted techniques that harness the power of comparatively large datasets in order to find patterns, quantify them descriptively or even simply check the presence of posited forms in the data. Perhaps one of the most prominent approaches one should mention is corpus-based discourse analysis, or CBDA (see, e.g., Baker 2006). A common criticism of close-reading approaches to discourse analysis is that they may be too deeply rooted in the researcher's pre-existing belief. CBDA makes a step towards the benchmark of empirical, unbiased investigation by relying more on quantified and reproducible findings.

Heinrich and Schäfer (2018: 135) emphasise the auxiliary role of the corpus, which should 'enable hermeneutic researchers to analyze and qualitatively interpret huge amounts of textual data without excessive cherry-picking'. Corpus-based discourse analysis typically involves obtaining concordances of search terms using corpus software, and manually analysing and interpreting them to uncover *discourse*: 'a set of meanings, metaphors, representations ... that in some way together produce a particular version of events' (Burr 1995: 48). This has been done for various issues and employing different datasets: some examples among many are Koteyko et al. (2008) for infectious diseases in UK media and government discourses, Dayter (2016) for self-representation of ballet apprentices online, Kim (2014) for the representation of North Korea in US media, Messerli and Locher (2021) for humour support in timed comments and Dayter and Rüdiger (2022) for manosphere discourses.

Another step towards the researcher's pre-existing taxonomies informed by literature, intuition and pilot studies is made in the family of analytical techniques known as corpus-assisted discourse studies (CADS). CADS research often relies on the critical discourse analysis framework and addresses politically laden issues, such as construction of race (Krishnamurthy 1996), discourse about the Iraq war in the press (Marchi & Taylor 2009) or representation of European citizenship (Bayley & Williams 2012). CADS differs from CBDA in respect to the degree of presuppositions and taxonomies that the researcher brings to the analysis. Love and Baker (2015), for instance, studied British Parliamentary arguments against LGBT equality and how they evolved over time. On the one hand, the method they used is very similar to classic CBDA. They started with a keyword analysis and a search for the collocates of the relevant terms to identify the salient lexical items in the debate, and then manually examined the concordances for these items. On the other hand, the choice of the search queries was informed by the purpose of the study: analysing the gradual shift from more to less explicit homophobic argumentation in the debates about same-sex marriage. Love and Baker (2015: 84) describe how their pre-existing agenda informed the study: 'knowing that the speakers ... voted against gay marriage, and that public attitudes towards homosexuality had altered enables a fuller interpretation and explanation of their language'.

Corpus-assisted approaches to pragmatics and discourse analysis present a multidimensional space, ranging from methods that combine traditional lexical corpus searches with qualitative analysis along pragmatic dimensions. While some scholars identify strongly with labels such as CADS or CBDA, the borders between the approaches are often fuzzy. In fact, different steps are often combined in a sequential or simultaneous manner in order to design the best methodology to answer a particular research question. In what follows, we will illustrate some of the possible combinations of methodological steps that allow the combination of qualitative and quantitative approaches in custom-made corpora. The advantage of this combination lies in arriving at patterns that are particular to the corpus in question by combining the results of different layers of analysis.

4.2 Case Studies: Scaffolded, Quantified Analysis of Online Health Practices

Scholars have many options when attempting to develop the best possible research design for their particular research interest. The examples we draw on here stem from research output that comes from a project entitled *Language and Health Online: Typing Yourself Healthy* (SNSF-funded[1]), which worked with custom-made corpora. The combined methods are:

(1) a content/thematic analysis, which establishes the aboutness and context of the texts,

(2) a discursive moves analysis, which establishes the compositional structure of the texts,

(3) a selective analysis of linguistic form and function of particular linguistic expressions in context,

(4) drawing on any type of further research steps that help us answer our research questions in more depth.

The first three steps (and the fourth to different degrees) are based on qualitative analysis that follows after codebook development and training in order to arrive at reproducibility and reliability of pragmatic patterns. With the help of corpus annotation software and corpus linguistics search methods, different layers of analysis can be brought together, as explained in what follows. The aim is to identify pragmatic patterns of communication that are valid for the corpus in question. This combination of methods is meant to illustrate only one possible approach and is not meant to claim exclusivity or novelty per se (since each of these steps exists independently from each other). However, this research design allowed us to arrive at meaningful insights about the practices in question which, crucially, also facilitated comparability and reproducibility.

To explain why the suggested steps and scaffolded approach was chosen for the *Language and Health Online* project, we first introduce its research aims and context. The general perspective we took was that of interpersonal

[1] We wish to thank the Swiss National Science Foundation for funding the project *Language and Health Online* (100016_143286/1).

pragmatics (Locher & Graham 2010), i.e. the study of how it matters who speaks to whom; what type of and how relationships are created, maintained and challenged through language use; and how these patterns can be linked to intersecting ideologies (such as gender, politeness, age). What is particularly at stake in communication in health contexts is the constructed and perceived expertise (be this of a biomedical and/or experiential kind) and the potential creation of trust (Locher & Schnurr 2017). In 2006, Locher published work on an online health-advice column, working with a custom corpus of 2,286 question–answer letters in an online archive of the site (990,000 words) (Locher 2006). From 2012–17, a project continued this research avenue by working on complementary datasets. Rudolf von Rohr (2015, 2017, 2018) explored the role of persuasion in a corpus on smoking cessation, which comprised thirty professional anti-smoking websites as well as peer-to-peer online fora for cessation support. Thurnherr (2017, 2022) worked on a smaller dataset of email counselling in short-term therapy to explore the creation of the therapeutic alliance. The data consisted of the full short therapy cycle of five clients with one counsellor. What these projects have in common is a joint research interest in exploring identity construction and the creation of expertise within interpersonal pragmatics (Rudolf von Rohr et al. 2019), and the application of a mixed methodology that combines insights from corpus linguistics with qualitative analysis inspired by the study of relational work. From a corpus linguistic perspective, all three corpora are small and custom-made, but they are large enough to warrant a quantified approach in order to arrive at the representative patterns for the individual corpora. The motivation to engage in quantification of qualitative analytic steps stems from the desire to achieve a more robust result of the general patterns within the corpus. The methodological orientation of the *Language and Health Online* project was described in Locher and Thurnherr (2017) after the completion of the project. In what follows, we reiterate and complement the observations made there in light of the purpose of this Element.

As our research questions on relational work in e-health needed a qualitative interpretation of linguistic surface structures in context, we proposed a layered analysis of data in order to answer the following questions (Locher & Thurnherr, 2017: 17):

(1) What characteristic activities are employed in the different e-health practices (e.g. conveying information, giving advice or reflecting on interact-
ants' interpretations of events or relationships, inviting introspection)?
(2) What linguistic strategies are employed to achieve these activities?

(3) What is the relation between the patterns of linguistic strategies and the creation of interpersonal effects (e.g. solidarity, empathy, power, the thera-peutic alliance, identity construction)?

In order to embed our analysis of the function of linguistic strategies (and not just their forms) in their context, we approached the corpora with the four steps mentioned at the beginning of this section: (1) a content/thematic analysis, (2) a discursive moves analysis, (3) a selective analysis of linguistic form and function of particular linguistic expressions in context and (4) drawing on a selection of further methods depending on the research question.

To illustrate this, first consider the analysis of *Lucy Answers*, a US health-advice column run by an educational institution. The data in this analysis consists of online advice entries in the form of a question letter by an advice-seeker and a response letter by an (invented) agony aunt. Table 2, reproduced from Locher (2006: 117), shows how the different layers of the analysis of the response letters are scaffolded. All of the levels were annotated with *Oxygen XML Editor*. The labels are mutually exclusive. In case of co-occurrence, combined tags were created (such as bonding-humour).

Step 1 was concerned with the overall topic of the entry, or the aboutness of the texts (on content/thematic analysis, see Guest et al. 2012; Saldaña 2013). In this case, the topic classification of the original data source was adopted from the archive that the source provides. This information later allowed for grouping of topics into biomedically oriented questions and more interpersonal-oriented topics.

Step 2 consisted of an analysis of the entire texts into their compositional units (often roughly one or more paragraphs) that contained so-called discursive moves, i.e. the 'kind of contribution that the entry made to the ongoing interchange' (Miller & Gergen 1998: 192). Rather than coding on the speech-act and sentence level, entire passages were coded in their overall contribution to the text composition (e.g. advice-giving, assessments, etc.). As advice-giving was the centre of analysis, it was then possible to see how the sequence of discursive moves prepares for advice-giving and to assess how this discursive move is embedded within the overall rhetoric of the text.

In Step 3, a selection of linguistic forms was systematically looked for and coded for their function. Since exploring advice-giving was the main aim of this study, an analysis of how the advisory sentences were syntactically realised (imperative, declarative, interrogative) was conducted (this was done within the advisory discursive move with an XML tag). In addition, a selection of rela-tional work strategies were systematically tagged, such as hedging or boosting. The codes were partly adopted from existing literature but also developed

Table 2 Categories for the analysis of problem and response letters of *Lucy Answers* (abbreviated and merged from Locher 2006: 117, 209)

Step 1	Step 2		Step 3
Topic category	**Content structure level**		**Relational work level**
drugs emotional	*Problem letter:* address		
health fitness/	unit (one or more)	apology comment on	appealing bonding
nutrition general health		previous record	boosting criticising
relationships sexual health		compliment explanation	hedging using humour in
sexuality		metacomment background	combination with the other rela-
		problem statement question	tional work levels
		request advice thanks	
	pseudonym		appeal humour
			neutral none
	Response letter: address		
	unit (one or more)	advice assessment	bonding boosting
		disclaimer explanation	criticising empathising
		farewell general information	hedging praising
		metacomment open category	using humour in combination with
		own experience referral	the other rela- tional work
			levels
	signature		

bottom-up. The interest was to find out which discursive moves contained which relational work strategies. One of the findings was that hedging did not only occur within the advisory discursive moves (saving the face of the advisee) but also within assessments (saving the face of the advisor).

In Step 4, widening the scope, a number of further corpus linguistic and non-corpus linguistic qualitative steps were undertaken. For example, interviews were conducted with the professional health team, a computer-assisted dia-chronic study was conducted that compared original and updated entries to see whether just biomedical content or also the style of the entries changed, and the creation of the advisor voice was explored with case studies.

This scaffolded analysis resulted in a nesting structure that allowed the researchers to ask which discursive moves (Step 2) contained particular rela-tional work strategies (Step 3), and to explore whether these realisations were topic sensitive (Step 1). This qualitative analysis was done for 10 per cent of the overall corpus, i.e. 280 question–answer letters, and made it possible to make robust statements about the patterns of the overall corpus. The codebooks, with definitions and illustrations of the codes, are included in the study and reliability of coding was achieved by testing the codebook with a group of peers.

The time it takes to establish a codebook can be substantial and needs to be taken into account in one's study design. Depending on your research question and approach, codebooks can draw on existing lists of codes (top-down), be developed from the data (bottom-up) or combine both possibilities. In all cases, reliability of codes and coding needs to be established. MacQueen et al. (2008) describe the cyclical development of a reliable codebook with a flow chart that shows how stable categories are developed before the entire dataset is analysed (see Figure 1).

Both Rudolf von Rohr (2018) and Thurnherr (2022) adopted and adapted these research steps to give justice to their data. They worked with the qualitative coding software *NVivo*. This software allows the coding of the same text passage with multiple codes and exploring co-coding (i.e. the layering of analysis). It also offers a function that establishes coder-agreement and has query options for cluster analysis of the codes and word frequency analysis, etc. Other commonly used qualitative coding software are for example MAXQDA and ATLAS.ti.

Rudolf von Rohr and Thurnherr first established what their texts are about in a qualitative analysis, secured with coder-agreement (Step 1, content/thematic analysis). The smoking cessation websites had different parts and sub-sites (e.g. facing quitting; inform on quitting; point out biomedical or lifestyle reasons to quit smoking; support) and the analysis was able to demonstrate the heterogen-eity of the dataset. The therapy email exchanges were classified according to the problems that were raised by the counselee and detected by the therapist (e.g. anxiety or depression).

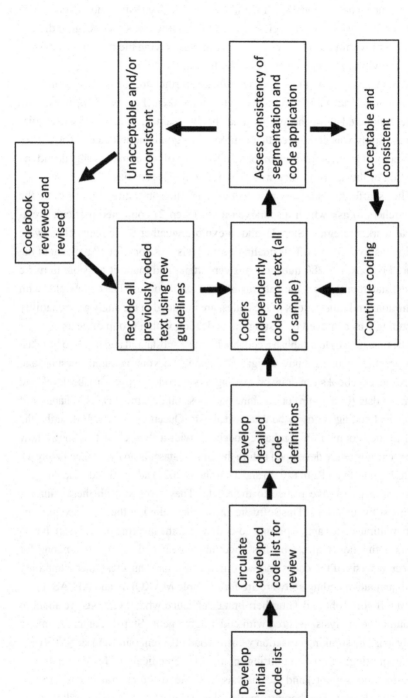

Figure 1 Codebook development (MacQueen et al. 2008: 128)

In Step 2, they developed their own set of discursive moves bottom-up to qualitatively analyse the composition of the texts. In the case of Rudolf von Rohr, this was done for a subcorpus of websites and peer-to-peer support fora; in the case of Thurnherr, for the entire counselling exchanges. The development of a codebook was established bottom-up and was thus data-driven. This was an important desideratum so as not to impose pre-existing notions on the texts. However, as both practices have an advisory core, similar discursive moves emerged. Consider Table 3, which shows the discursive moves for Locher (2006), Rudolf von Rohr (2018) and Thurnherr (2022). Comparable discursive moves appear in the same row. The table also shows that there are discursive moves unique to particular datasets, such the 'Official forum welcome' for the fora, or the 'Introductory message' written by the counsellor in the email therapy exchanges. Some of the discursive moves are only used by some interactors (e.g. problem letter writers (PL) versus response letter writers (RL) in *Lucy Answers*, thread initiators (I) vs post-respondents (R) in the forum data, or client (C) vs therapist (T) in the email therapy corpus). The discursive move analysis in combination with Step 1 thus allows scholars to find nuanced similarities and differences between comparable datasets. One of our findings is that the number of discursive moves to describe the practices in question is actually rather small within this advisory field, a result also confirmed by other studies that adopted a similar approach with discursive moves (see, e.g., DeCapua & Dunham 2012; Morrow 2012; Placencia 2012).

Looking at the realisation of relational work (Step 3), we found that it does not only matter how the advisory passages are linguistically realised (e.g. by exploring linguistic mitigation devices) but also how these passages are embedded within the overall composition of the texts, often resulting in mitigating effects.

In Step 4, widening the scope, Rudolf von Rohr (2018: ch. 6) explored how particular datasets clustered according to their use of discursive moves, drawing on the NVivo query options. Since her thirty websites differed in their multimodal composition, the computer-assisted analysis helped to find patterns. Thurnherr (2022) interviewed the counsellor who provided her data and organised workshops with counsellors to discuss results and to learn from the insights of the counsellors about their chosen strategies. She also drew on corpus linguistics tools such as word frequency and collocation analyses to explore the composition of discursive moves.

4.3 Conclusion

In all three studies of the *Language and Health Online* project, the computer-assisted qualitative data analysis software (CAQDAS) was crucial for the

Table 3 Types of discursive moves used to analyse *Lucy Answers* (Locher 2006), smoking cessation website modules and fora (Rudolf von Rohr 2018) and email counselling (Thurnherr 2022) in alphabetical order

Lucy Answers PL = problem letter; RL = response letter	Website modules	Email counselling I = thread initiator; R = respondent	Forum interaction C = client; T = therapist
Advice (RL)	Advice	Advice (I, R)	Advice-giving (T)
Apology (PL)		Apology (I, R)	Apology (C, T)
Assessment (RL)	Assessment	Assessment (I, R)	Assessment (C, T)
Background information (PL)		Background information (I)	
Comment on previous record (PL)			
Compliment (PL)			
Disclaimer (RL)			
Explanation (PL, RL)	Explanation		
Farewell (RL)		Farewell (I, R)	Farewell (C, T)
General information (RL)	General information		General information (T)
Address (PL, RL)	Header	Greeting (I, R)	Greeting (C, T)
			Introductory message (T)
Metacomment (PL, RL)	Metacomment		Metacomment (C, T)

Prediction
Other voice

Own experience (RL)
Problem statement (PL)

Question (PL)
Referral (RL)
Request advice (PL)

Thanks (PL)

Official forum welcome (R)

Own experience (I)

Quote (I, R)

Request advice or information (I, R)

Thanks (I, R)
Welcoming (I, R)
Well-wishing (I, R)

Problem statement (C)
Quoting (C, T)

Referral (T)
Request for advice (C)

Request for information (T)
Scheduling (C, T)
Thanks (C, T)

analysis (in our case *Oxygen XML Editor* and *NVivo*). It allowed the researchers to quantify and keep track of the qualitative analytic steps and, importantly, to explore the results of the scaffolded design of the methodology. A big advantage of qualitative coding software such as *ATLAS.ti*, *CATMA*, *MAXQDA* or *NVivo* is therefore that multiple coding of the same string is possible and that clustering can be explored. In addition, software such as *AntConc*, *Wordsmith Tools* or *SPSS* can complement the corpus analysis with frequency, keywords and collocation analyses.

The analysis is informed by results from previous work as well as by the data itself. Developing the codebooks in pilot studies not only allows the establishment of coder-agreement but it also gives justice to the data since codes can be detected that are novel and unique to a particular dataset. The persistence of the analytic coding in the corpus also allows explorations that were not originally on the research agenda. For example, complementary to our own research interests, we explored a comparative perspective upon invitation. In Thurnherr et al. (2016), we explored our individual corpora top-down in order to explore narrative passages in our different datasets, and in Rudolf von Rohr and Locher (2020), we pursued the use of complimenting. In both cases, our bottom-up analysis of discursive moves had not yielded these particular concerns as primary, i.e. we did not create a discursive move for these units on their own (but complimenting was included as a relational work category in Locher 2006); however, we were able to reinterpret our previous analysis with the help of lexical searches of the corpora and then link the results to the discursive moves in which narrative passages and compliments occur. In other words, previous analysis can be combined with the exploration of new research interests.

The analyses discussed here in the context of the *Language and Health Online* project are fundamentally based on qualitative interpretation of lexical strings in context, but this process is quantified. The benefits of the quantification and scaffolding lie in being able to establish reproducible patterns that are representative for the corpus in question. It should not be denied that much of the time invested in this kind of exploration goes into establishing coder-agreement (MacQueen et al. 2008), which, however, is worth it in order to arrive at robust results.

Our brief introduction to the *Language and Health Online* project just described one of many possible ways to work with a custom-made corpus to gauge pragmatic research questions by drawing on and combining corpus linguistic methodologies and the possibilities of layered annotation. Other corpus-assisted studies (see Section 4.1 for a selection) make use of different corpus linguistics tools in order to do pragmatic analyses. Key to all of these endeavours is that the corpus-assisted approach to pragmatics aims at combining qualitative with quantitative steps of analysis. Referring to a corpus in a replicable and systematic way enables the creation of taxonomies, ensuring their descriptive adequacy and allowing us to validate them empirically.

5 Compatibility and Comparability: Combining Existing Corpora

5.1 Introduction

Working with a combination of several corpora can take different forms. In many cases, researchers access each corpus individually and compare results, for instance on the basis of normalised frequencies. In other cases, existing corpus resources are combined into a new corpus. There are many reasons why researchers may want to work with several corpora at once. For instance, they may be interested in comparing different varieties of a language or different languages by using a corpus for each language or language variety. Perhaps they want to carry out a diachronic study by comparing corpora from different periods. They may want to make comparisons across different domains by working with several domain-specific corpora. Or they may simply want to base their observations on a larger set of data by combining different corpora.

This last point is particularly relevant for historical studies (see also Brinton 2012). Whereas researchers interested in present-day language usually have the option of expanding the data that is available to them by collecting more data, this is often not the case for historical studies. Here, research is limited to texts that have survived and, at least for the earliest periods of English, most of these have already been included into the corpora we have available today. For instance, the *Dictionary of Old English Corpus* (*DOE*) includes almost all surviving texts from the Old English period, amounting to roughly 3 million words of Old English. For slightly later periods of English, such as Late Middle English and Early Modern English, material not included in existing corpora can still be found in archives, but access restrictions to such material and the nature of the data mean that transforming it into electronic corpus data is usually an extremely time-intensive process. As a consequence, it often takes entire teams of researchers working on such corpora for several years before the data is ready to work with. Thus, instead of compiling a new, larger corpus, it makes sense to build on the work that has already been carried out by working with several existing corpora in combination.

However, working with several corpora side-by-side brings with it a range of challenges. These challenges can be summarised under two different headings: compatibility and comparability. With compatibility we refer to formal and technical aspects, ranging from the way in which corpus data is edited and stored, how it can be accessed and searched, and what metainformation is available. These aspects influence how researchers can work with different corpora side-by-side and how easy or difficult it is to retrieve the same kind of information from different corpora – or whether this is in fact impossible. For instance, if one of two corpora includes syntactic annotation, but the other does not, comparisons across these corpora that rely on syntactic annotation cannot be made. With comparability, we refer to differences in the data that are included in the corpora, as well as to differences in the calculation methods of corpus tools. While compatibility issues affect whether or not information can be retrieved from all corpora used in a given study, comparability issues affect whether or not the retrieved information can be compared across corpora in a meaningful way. For instance, if two corpora include syntactic annotation, but the way in which syntactic units were classified differs across the two corpora, then the results may not be comparable, because they are influenced by differences in the annotation schemes. Researchers need to know their corpora extremely well in order to be aware of differences across the corpus data that affect their results and interpretations. Compatibility and comparability of corpora are challenges that all corpus linguists face when they work with different corpora. They are not restricted to corpus pragmatics, but, of course, they need to be addressed when studying pragmatic features with corpora.

In the remainder of this section, we first discuss issues of compatibility (Section 5.2) and comparability (Section 5.3). In Section 5.4, we then present a study that is based on a combination of different Early Modern English corpora to illustrate some of these issues in more detail.

5.2 Compatibility

When starting to work with different corpora, practical problems often appear quite early on. Unless the corpora are provided by the same research team or included on the same platform, even gaining access to the corpus data may take very different forms. Some corpora are available for full-text downloads, some can be copied from CD-ROMs and others can only be accessed through online search interfaces. This last option involves most restrictions. Researchers have to rely on the corpus tools that are provided by the online interface, and they cannot reprocess data, for instance by applying their own part-of-speech tagging. If different corpora have to be accessed through different search interfaces, it is possible that different tools are offered on the two sites, or – perhaps even worse – that the tools appear to be the same, but that they apply different methods. Unfortunately, not all corpus interfaces document in a clear and transparent way how they operate, and differences in calculation methods can have profound effects on comparability (see Section 5.3).

For corpora that are available as full-text versions, gaining an overview of the corpus files, their format and how they can be processed is sometimes not straightforward. There are corpora that come as collections of folders and files with an intuitive structure, such as folders and files per text type or period. Others, like the downloadable version of the *Movie Corpus*, are presented in the form of huge text files with no apparent order of the data and only minimal metainformation in the form of a numerical ID within the text files, which has to be cross-checked in an Excel file. While such information can be processed by computers, this form of presentation makes it harder for researchers to understand the structure of the data. In addition, many corpora are available in different versions: ordered by text type or period (e.g. *ARCHER*), as text only, part-of-speech tagged or parsed (e.g. *Parsed Corpus of Early English Correspondence* (*PCEEC*)), with or without spelling normalisation (e.g. *Early Modern English Medical Texts* (*EMEMT*)), or with or without annotation (*CED*). Researchers need to know a great deal about all the corpora they want to work with in order to choose the corpus version that best fits their needs.

Perhaps the biggest practical problem for downloadable corpora is posed by different file formats. Nowadays, the most common format by far is XML, but there are still corpora that are available in other formats. Especially for older corpora, text files with custom-made annotation formats are not uncommon. Even if all corpora are available in XML format, different corpora often use different conventions with respect to the tagset and presentation of metainformation. The Text Encoding Initiative (TEI) has developed extensive guidelines and recommendations on how to present various kinds of text material in digital form based on XML. However, while these conventions have been applied in some corpus projects, many compilers still decide to develop their own annotation scheme, custom-tailored towards their corpus data and the needs of their study. When working with corpora in different formats, researchers need to decide whether or not to transform all of them into one single format. This process can be time-consuming, and it can also involve the loss of metainformation. The advantage is, however, that the corpora can then be processed in the same way, which makes the analysis easier and improves the comparability of the results.

One way of dealing with compatibility problems is by removing most metainformation from a corpus and treating it as a collection of text material that can be further processed with a given set of corpus tools. This is what multi-corpus tools like the commercially available *Sketch Engine* often do. *Sketch Engine* is an online interface that provides access to the content of 600 corpora in more than ninety languages. While this means that researchers can gain access to a dazzling amount of data, much of the metainformation of the individual corpora is lost and the access to the corpus texts is strictly limited by the search interface.

This poses serious problems for the interpretation of results. Especially for studies that rely on qualitative interpretations of retrieved instances, such platforms are of very limited use. For pragmatic studies, for which access to contextual information is crucial, this approach is usually not suitable.

Even when corpora are prepared by researchers themselves, the goal of achieving compatibility without sacrificing richness of information is often not easy to achieve. Different types of data sometimes simply require different types of formatting and metainformation. For instance, for a corpus of drama texts, it is quite important to be able to distinguish between speaker labels, lines that are spoken by characters and stage directions. In contrast, such annotations make little sense for a corpus of newspaper data. However, in the latter, it may be important to distinguish between up-, mid- and down-market newspapers, between hard news articles and opinion pieces, and between headlines and the main body of an article (see, for instance, Landert 2014). For research questions for which such annotations play a role, decisions need to be taken with respect to how much annotation is retained. Retaining annotations may provide additional information for the interpretation of pragmatic functions and distributions, while at the same time making the datasets less compatible.

While this section has illustrated challenges with respect to compatibility of the formal and technical aspects of the corpora, Section 5.3 illustrates the challenges encountered with respect to comparability, i.e. whether the data that is included in and retrieved from the corpora is comparable.

5.3 Comparability

Comparability becomes an issue at two different levels: the level of the data that is included in a corpus (e.g. which registers, period, speakers, etc.) and the methods that are used to process the corpus data (e.g. how frequencies and collocations are calculated). The first of these issues is perhaps the more obvious one. For instance, if we want to make a comparison across two language varieties – e.g. British English and American English – by using a corpus for each variety, we need to be sure that the corpora are as similar to each other as possible in terms of corpus composition. This means that they should include the same proportion of texts from given registers, text types and language users. If this is not the case, any difference in corpus composition may distort the results. While this is an obvious point, it poses many practical problems, given that close similarity of composition is often not given.

There are various corpus projects that try to maximise comparability of corpus data across different varieties and/or time periods. Examples are the *Brown* and Lancaster–Oslo/Bergen (*LOB*) family of corpora, which consist of a set of corpora of American English (*Brown*) and British English (*LOB*). The original corpora, which included data from 1961, were complemented with comparable corpora from 1991/1992. Additional corpus components from later and earlier periods are published, and others are currently being compiled. For spoken language, the *BNClab* platform provides access to two subsets from the original *BNC1994* and the new *BNC2014*, which include demographically sampled data that can be used for sociolinguistic studies of language change. Another project that tries to maximise comparability of corpus data across different varieties of English is the *ICE* (see also Section 2.2). It consists of twenty-six corpora – some completed, some still in progress – each devoted to a different variety of English. Each corpus is compiled according to the same design principles, e.g. including 300 text samples of spoken and 200 samples of written language, which are spread across different genres (such as classroom lessons, broadcast discussions, parliamentary debates) in predefined ways (see www.ice-corpora.uzh.ch/en/design.html). However, in practical terms, some differences in corpus composition still occur even between these corpora. Some differences are related to the fact that some types of texts are not produced or not accessible in a given variety (e.g. parliamentary debates in the English of Malta, see Hilbert and Krug 2010: 60). Other differences are introduced through the duration of the project: while the British component of the corpus, *ICE-GB*, was compiled in the 1990s, new components are still in the process of being compiled, which means that data is collected about twenty-five years later than for the first corpus. Thus, with respect to time period, the corpora are not perfectly comparable.

In historical corpora, the kind of precision of comparability that the *ICE* offers can hardly be achieved. There are very practical limitations to corpus composition in the form of lack of surviving and accessible data. Moreover, text types and genres change over time, meaning that diachronic corpora spanning a long period cannot have exactly the same structural composition (see Taavitsainen 2016). For instance, in the *Helsinki Corpus*, 'drama comedy', 'trial proceedings' and 'personal diaries' are not included for Old and Middle English, because they either did not exist in, did not survive or were not accessible from these periods. In addition, text types and genres undergo development, too, so that texts from the same genre can include different linguistic characteristics at different points in time not because language overall has changed, but as a reflection of the development of the genre. For instance, Kohnen (1997) showed in an early study of the *Helsinki Corpus* that the increase of gerund constructions with direct object in the corpus section 'fiction' can be explained by the development of narrative prose, which resulted in longer and more complex fictional texts over time. Thus, the text category 'fiction' in the fifteenth century is quite different from the category 'fiction' in the seventeenth century. Given the context-dependency of pragmatic meaning, changes in text types and genres are likely to affect pragmatic forms and functions at least as much as lexical and grammatical characteristics.

Such differences in genre development and corpus composition across periods can have considerable effects on the results of linguistic studies, and they need to be taken into account for the interpretation. More problematic than known differences in corpus composition, therefore, are differences of which researchers are not aware. Familiarising oneself with the content and structure of a corpus is one of the most important steps in any corpus-pragmatic study.

When working with multiple corpora, it is highly advisable to either work with the full-text version of each corpus locally or to access them through the same interface – assuming that all corpora were processed identically on a given platform. If one has to rely on different corpus tools for different sets of data, there is always a danger that differences in the tools lead to different results, due to differences in calculation methods. To give an example, word counts can be calculated in many different ways: treating hyphenated words as one or two words, counting numbers as words or not, or whether or not to include punctuation in the word count. Such differences in how word counts are calculated can distort normalised frequencies. Frequency normalisation is a crucial step when working with several corpora. All results need to be presented in relation to the overall size of the corpus, which happens by dividing the number of instances retrieved from a corpus by the total number of words in the corpus. If the way in which word counts are calculated differs across different corpora, then frequency normalisation is affected and the normalised frequencies are no longer comparable.

In order to illustrate the variation in word count, Table 4 gives an overview of eight different results for the overall number of words in the *Sydney Corpus of Television Series*, four each for the non-standardised (*SydTV*) and partly standardised (*SydTV-Std*) version of the corpus. These results are provided by

Table 4 Number of words in the *Sydney Corpus of Television Dialogue*, according to corpus documentation (Bednarek 2018: 253)

Token definitions (Wordsmith 'tokens in text')	SydTV	SydTV-Std
hyphens do not separate words; ' not allowed within word	275,074	276,899
hyphens separate words; ' not allowed within words	276,287	278,112
hyphens do not separate words; ' allowed within word	258,944	260,824
hyphens separate words; ' allowed within word	260,157	262,037

Table 5 Word counts of the *Sydney Corpus of Television Dialogue* on *CQPweb* interface

	SydTV	*SydTV-Std*
Sydney Corpus of Television Dialogue	334,379	335,087
Sydney Corpus of television Dialogue CLAWS	334,998	335,223

Bednarek (2018: 253), who compiled the corpus, and they include an unusual amount of detailed information with respect to how they were calculated.

As these numbers show, even within the same corpus version, word counts can vary for around 5 per cent depending on how hyphens and apostrophes are treated. In addition to these differences, Table 5 shows four additional results for the word counts of the same corpus as they are provided on *CQPweb*, the interface through which the corpus can be accessed. Again, there are some differences between the version using the CLAWS tagset and the other version. More importantly, though, the numbers differ from those given by Bednarek (2018) by about 20 per cent. According to Bednarek (personal communication), this difference is due to differences in the treatment of multi-word units and punctuation.

The point here is not to assess which method of establishing word counts is the correct or the best method, but rather to raise awareness that such differences in establishing word counts can seriously distort results when comparing results derived from datasets that use different tokenisation methods. As a consequence, it is highly advisable to use the same methods and tools on all sets of data.

5.4 Case Study: Combining Four Early Modern English Corpora

This section illustrates some of the issues that arise when working with several corpora side-by-side by referring to a research project on epistemic stance in Early Modern English (Landert 2019). The main research of the project was based on four existing corpora: the *Corpus of English Dialogues 1560–1760* (*CED*), the *Early Modern English Medical Texts* corpus (*EMEMT*), the *Lampeter Corpus of Early English Tracts* (*LC*) and the *Parsed Corpus of Early English Correspondence* (*PCEEC*). These four topic- and domain-specific corpora are mid-sized, ranging from 1.2 to 2.2 million words, and all four corpora had been compiled with a great deal of care and extensive documentation with the aim of making it possible for other researchers to use them. Despite these ideal conditions, working with the corpora was not without problems.

Several of the corpora were available in more than one version, which made it necessary to decide which corpus version to use. For instance, the *EMEMT* was available in a version with normalised spelling and in a non-normalised version. For many parts of the analysis, using the normalised version would have been an advantage, since it would have removed the need to take spelling variation into account when formulating search terms. However, given that not all the corpora were available with normalised spelling, the non-normalised version was chosen in order to maintain comparability of the results. For the *PCEEC*, the corpus release that was available was based on the parsed version of the corpus, but for the project, the text-only version was used. While several of the corpora included versions with part-of-speech tagging, it was not clear to what extent the tagging was comparable between the corpora and, therefore, the text-only version without any linguistic tagging was used for all four corpora. For the study in question, no part-of-speech tagging was applied.

One aspect in which it was not possible to make the corpora comparable was time span. While all four corpora included Early Modern English data, they differed quite considerably with respect to the period they covered (see Figure 2). While the *PCEEC* starts in 1410, including some material from Late Middle English, the *LC* starts only in 1640, overlapping with the *PCEEC* for merely fifty-five years. Reducing the material to just the time span that is covered by all four corpora would have restricted the data too much. As a consequence, the entire corpora were included in the analysis, but the difference in coverage was considered during the interpretation.

Compatibility of corpus formats provided the biggest practical obstacle by far. Only one of the corpora, the *CED*, was available in XML format. This corpus was kept in XML, but some aspects of the annotation scheme were adjusted in order to facilitate later steps in the analysis. For instance, the name of the document-level tag was changed from <diaolgueDoc> to <document>, which was a tag that could be used for all four corpora. In this way, the same XPath query could be used to search all corpora. In addition, some

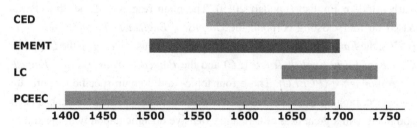

Figure 2 Time span of four Early Modern English corpora (*CED = Corpus of English Dialogues 1560–1760*; *EMEMT = Early Modern English Medical Texts* corpus; *LC = Lampeter Corpus of Early English Tracts*; *PCEEC = Parsed Corpus of Early English Correspondence*)

metainformation was integrated into the <document> tag in the form of attributes, such as the corpus section and the period of the text. Encoding this information as attribute made it possible to use it as filter criteria of XPath queries when searching the corpus.

The other three corpora had to be transformed to XML first. The *EMEMT* was transformed from an ASCII text version, the *PCEEC* from an HTML version and the *LC* from an SGML version – a format that was very innovative at the time the corpus was compiled but which proved to require quite some manual work for the transformation.

Irrespective of the format, the kind of information that was annotated differed considerably, due in part to differences in the nature of the data. To the extent that they described aspects of the data that were relevant for the analysis, many of these differences were retained, such as the distinction between speech representation and non-speech representation in the *CED*. Some types of information were considered not to be central for the scope of the project and these were removed whenever they would have introduced additional complexity into the data. For instance, the *LC* included very detailed information about the layout of the printed tracts, which was not taken into account in the analysis.

Following the transformation of the corpora to compatible XML versions, the four corpora were processed with the same tools, scripts and methods. In this way, the comparability of the results from the corpora was maximised. Potential effects on the results that were related to the corpus composition, the nature of the historical data, and genre- and text-type specific factors were considered throughout the interpretation. Some information about subsequent steps of the analysis are given in Section 6.4.

5.5 Conclusion

Combining different corpora in a single study can greatly enhance the available data and it can also open up research perspectives that could not be pursued with any single corpus on its own. At the same time, working with resources that were compiled at different times by different researchers with different research questions in mind and which can sometimes only be accessed by using different interfaces and tools creates a range of challenges. While any researcher who works with a corpus should know their corpus well, this is probably even more true for researchers who work with several different corpora in combination. By familiarising oneself very well with a corpus, its composition, its formatting and the tools that may come along with it, many problems that may affect the results can be identified and, ideally, avoided.

6 Scalability: Meaningful Pragmatics with Large Data

6.1 Processing Time and Corpus Size

Scalability as we use it in this section, refers to the ease with which a given method can be transferred to other, especially larger, corpora. Given the overall tendency of corpora to increase in size, it is worthwhile to discuss scalability and its consequences for quantitative and qualitative corpus methods. The factor that affects scalability most of all is the question of how the processing time a method requires relates to corpus size. It is important to note that processing time here refers not only to the processing time of computers. It involves all the steps involved in arriving at the result, from accessing the corpus and formulating queries, to reviewing and analysing results. In practical terms, computer processing time is negligible nowadays for most of the typical corpus pragmatic methods. The processing power of computers has increased a great deal and, as a consequence, the automatic computation of results has become a smaller part of the overall process, as far as duration is concerned. Thus, the other steps in the process tend to decide how processing time increases in relation to corpus size.

For the majority of the quantitative corpus methods that are most often used in corpus pragmatics – such as normalised frequencies, frequent collocations, n-grams and keywords – the automatic computation of results is so quick that the overall time needed for the analysis hardly increases with corpus size. For instance, if we want to calculate normalised frequencies based on a huge corpus, all we need are the number of words in the corpus and the number of instances we are interested in. As long as these two numbers are returned automatically by the corpus tools, we have the results within seconds of entering our query, even if the query is run on a very large corpus. When applying restrictions on queries that go beyond searches for strings, such as part-of-speech tags or lemma searches, queries can become noticeably slower for large corpora. Still, in most cases, queries will return results in under a minute, often even in under ten seconds. For instance, the calculation examples provided by Davies on the 1.9 billion word *Corpus of Global Web-Based English* (*GloWbE*) corpus for queries including lemma searches and part-of-speech tagged elements all range from two to seven seconds (www.english-corpora.org/speed.asp). Thus, while the computer processing time of calculating the number of instances will increase with corpus size, the overall duration of the process is so short that it hardly matters in practical terms.

For other common corpus operations, such as for the calculation of collocations and keywords, the increase of computer processing time with corpus size may be more noticeable. For very large corpora, computer processing time can become an issue for such operations. However, in practical terms, corpus infrastructures often offer solutions to deal with such issues, for instance by including pre-calculations of word frequencies that speed up the process.

However, the situation changes drastically when we turn to qualitative analysis. Methods that require researchers to analyse each result manually have very poor scalability for very large corpora. If the number of relevant instances increases with corpus size, then the amount of time to analyse these instances increases in a linear fashion as well. For rare linguistic phenomena, very large corpora are still an advantage, but even for moderately frequent phenomena, large corpora can soon produce more results than a researcher can analyse in a qualitative manner. This means that larger corpora are not always an advantage for such studies. Although they may include more potentially valuable material for qualitative analysis, finding it in the mass of data may become very difficult.

In the remainder of this section, we will discuss some old and new approaches to this challenge and we will discuss options for making the most out of large amounts of corpus data, even for studies that require a great deal of qualitative analysis. We will first discuss sampling, as a well-established way of dealing with large sets of retrieved hits, before turning to more recent approaches that aim at retrieving texts or passages of texts from a corpus that can provide particularly rich insight into a given pragmatic phenomenon.

6.2 Sampling

A popular approach to limit the number of person-hours spent on manually annotating pragmatic phenomena is to use a small section of the entire corpus, i.e. a sample. The assumption behind sampling is that the sample is sufficiently representative of the entire corpus for the researcher to be able to generalise the findings to the corpus, and consequently, to the larger population. It is of crucial importance to base sampling on systematic decisions rather than convenience in order to make sure that the sample includes the full range of variability in the population (Biber 1993). These decisions will depend on the type of corpus in question and always need to be carefully documented.

The same sampling principles apply to choosing a subsample from our corpus as from the population at large: in corpus linguistics, researchers traditionally resort either to simple random sampling or to stratified sampling. To conduct random sampling, the analyst numbers the sampling units in the collection (most commonly, individual corpus files in the corpus) and chooses the sample using a random numbers generator. The drawback of this method is that the resulting sample might not include relatively rare items in the corpus, since the chance of an item being chosen correlates with its frequency in the corpus (McEnery et al. 2005).

Stratified sampling can alleviate this problem by sampling from various parts of the corpus in a balanced way. When sampling from a population, we first divide it into homogenous groups, or strata, according to a chosen principle: for example, demographic strata such as age and gender of the speaker. Data from each stratum is then sampled randomly. When drawing a subsample from a corpus, it is of course possible to rely on some aspects of the pre-existing sampling frame as strata. For instance, Maynard and Leicher (2007: 111) created a subsample of the *Michigan Corpus of Academic Spoken English* (*MICASE*) corpus for their pragmatic annotation project by selecting fifty transcripts from the total of 152 transcripts based on the original sampling category 'academic division' (humanities and arts, physical sciences and engineering, etc.).

One limitation of choosing the subsample for manual pragmatic annotation in this manner is that the sampling frame of a corpus may not fit the present research question. In that case, the researcher may choose a different stratification principle that would result in a more adequate sample. In pragmatic research, meaningful strata are often thematic, although structural criteria such as the number of discourse participants, the length of corpus file or the time of production are also used. An instance of this process is the study of illocutionary acts in SMS by Sotillo (2012), who sampled 1,217 text messages from her overall corpus of 5,809 messages by dividing the subsets of data donated by each study participant into three groups chronologically ('beginning', 'middle' and 'end' of the 1.5 year period of data collection) and then randomly sampling from these three categories.

Finally, two considerations to keep in mind concern the sampling unit and sample size. These should be based on the careful consideration of the research question, although convenience may drive the decision to keep the pre-existing sampling unit and to minimise the size of the sample to be annotated. While many corpora are built around the unit of an entire text or a speech event, a more meaningful choice for a pragmatic study might be to sample only the beginnings of texts or only the turns by one interlocutor (as, for instance, Weisser (2018: 271) observed that greetings occur predominantly in the beginnings and ends of the Switchboard corpus files). The choice of the sampling unit and the sampling process itself can indeed become a powerful tool in optimising the annotation efficiency, as Sections 6.3 and 6.4 will demonstrate.

6.3 Case Study: Manual Identification of High-Density Corpus Files for the Study of Self-Praise

This section addresses the speech act of self-praise: an expressive speech act that gives credit to the speaker for some attribute which is positively valued by the speaker and the potential audience (Dayter 2016: 65). While linguistic approaches to politeness prior to the discursive turn described self-praise as face-threatening and inappropriate, recently it has been recognised as an integral part of communication across a wide variety of communicative contexts (Matley 2017; Dayter 2018).

'Self-praise' and associated metapragmatic labels such as 'bragging' or 'boasting' are negatively charged and seldom used. This speech act, which also lacks stable IFIDs and metacommunicative expressions, is difficult to extract from large corpora using any of the three methods mentioned in Section 1.4.[2] At the same time, the empirical study of self-praise using corpus approaches remains crucial for the adequate description of this long-neglected speech act.

The first steps towards identifying self-praise in a corpus used fully manual annotation (Dayter 2016) and semi-automatic annotation through a list of candidate IFIDs (Dayter 2018). However, such approaches are not easily scalable to large datasets. An alternative approach to identifying this pragmatic phenomenon, aiming to be scalable, is described in Dayter (2021). The driving assumption behind the method is that even in the corpora that are relatively homogenous in terms of genre, some text excerpts may be richer in the pragmatic phenomenon in question than others. To give a somewhat trivial example, if we are interested in a study of greetings, it would be efficient to limit our manual annotation to the first few turns of every conversation included in a corpus of spoken interactions. Although such an approach might miss some untypical instances of greetings (for example, when an interlocutor joins a conversation well underway), it will nevertheless achieve high sensitivity and save the human annotator the significant effort of closely reading the remaining bulk of corpus texts.

The speech act of self-praise does not immediately offer such a convenient springboard to limit the search. It is, however, conceivable that self-praise might occur more frequently in some subtypes of speech events than in others. In order to test this hypothesis, Dayter (2021) conducted a pilot annotation of her domain-specific 230,000 words corpus. The corpus included seventy-two speech events in high-level political contexts that were predominantly monologic and delivered in the one-to-many modality: addresses at the United Nations (UN) General Assembly, UN Security Council, UN Human Rights Council and UN Universal Periodic Review sessions, as well as statement sections of presidential and ministerial press-conferences. The study established that self-praise by politicians overwhelmingly occurs in a certain kind of oral report. This is a specific United Nations rhetorical subgenre (the

---

[2] The three methods are (1) the search for IFIDs, (2) the search for known lexico-grammatical patterns and (3) the study of metacommunicative expressions (see Section 1.4).

statement section of the Universal Periodic Review (UPR) of the human rights records of the UN member states) which calls for the speaker to report on their latest achievements. Although other speech events in the corpus similarly offer speakers an opportunity to present their activities in a positive light, UPR reports emerged as the locus of self-praise.

In order to catch as many instances of self-praise as possible, annotation was conducted in two rounds. The first round relied on semi-automatic identification of self-praise excerpts through search queries using candidate IFIDs (such as *the best*, *the most*, *leading*) and metapragmatic commentary (such as *praise*). The retrieved concordance lines were manually checked to confirm the presence of self-praise.

Although combining IFIDs with metapragmatic remarks is a fairly successful approach in detecting explicit and/or direct self-praise (Example 6.1), this speech act is often performed implicitly and indirectly (Example 6.2, which is impossible to recognise as self-praise without the detailed understanding of the co-text), or directly, but using creative lexical items (Example 6.3).

(6.1) Belarus has the best indicator in the CIS region in the level of child mortality (0009EnTr)

(6.2) we have also submitted an interim report on the review of implementing the recommendations made at the end of the first UPR (0009EnTr)

(6.3) I believe America is exceptional in part because we've shown a willingness through this sacrifice of blood and treasure to stand up not only for own narrow self-interest but also for the interest of all (0002RuTr)

Consequently, every speech event where self-praise had been detected in the first round of extraction was manually annotated to catch the instances of self-praise not marked by IFIDs or metapragmatic expressions. After reviewing the distribution of self-praise across the corpus files, three files emerged as especially dense in self-praise. All of these belonged to the category of statements within the Universal Periodic Review. All in all, twelve transcripts of speech events out of the total seventy-two events in the corpus contained self-praise. Six of these belong to the category of UPR statements and, as Figure 3 demonstrates, are much denser in self-praise (highlighted) than other subgenres.

To sum up, further self-praise research on UN political discourse involving manual annotation of the highly interpretative category of self-praise (for example, following the corpus-assisted methodology outlined in Section 4 of this Element) can be conducted more efficiently if the annotators' efforts are limited to the UPR statements. Although this example concerns a relatively small spoken corpus, Section 6.4 describes the successful adoption of the principle to

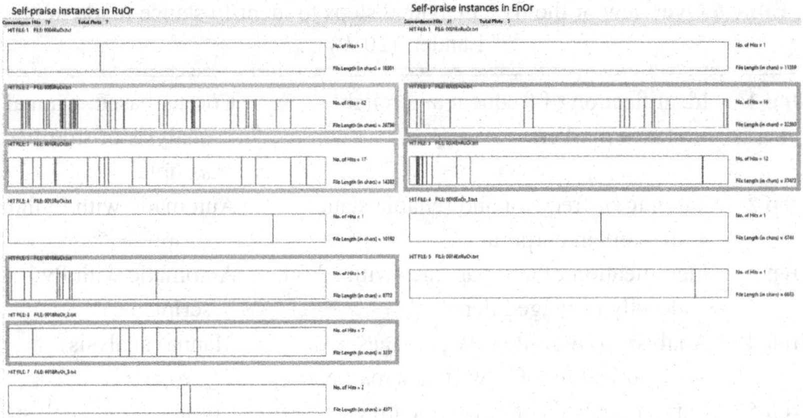

Figure 3 Concordance plot of self-praise distribution in the corpus of political discourse, adapted from Dayter (2021: 34), produced in AntConc 3.5.0. UPR statements are highlighted with frames (RuOr: Russian Original; EnOr: English Original).

automatically identify high-density passages in a much larger corpus and thus scale the study of a pragmatic phenomenon to a corpus of many million words.

6.4 Case Study: Automatic Extraction of High-Density Passages of Epistemic Stance in Early Modern English

Pragmatic phenomena tend to cluster not just in certain text documents but even in certain passages of documents. For instance, for requests, Culpeper and Archer (2008) identify a tendency of using multiple requests in the same turn for their data from Early Modern English trials and, to a lesser extent, in drama. Likewise, Archer and Gillings (2020), in their study of lying and deception in Shakespeare's plays, note that deceptive features tend to occur in clusters. Vaughan et al. (2017) find that certain items of vague language tend to co-occur. And, as Andersen (2011: 601) points out, studies have repeatedly found that discourse markers tend to cluster together with other discourse markers (see also Aijmer 2013). So far, this tendency of pragmatic features to cluster together has often been identified as a result of linguistic studies. Only rarely have clusters been taken as the starting point of linguistic methods. By developing methods that identify clusters of related pragmatic features in texts, we can complement existing approaches.

For instance, if we know that pragmatic features have a tendency to cluster together, we can use this fact in order to develop analytical steps that allow us to identify and extract passages in corpora that contain such

Table 6 Overview of the five analytical steps to identify stance markers in Landert (2019)

Step 1	Identification of frequent and reliable stance markers	Corpus-based, manual analysis of stratified sample
Step 2	Tagging of frequent and reliable stance markers in corpora	Automatic with Python script
Step 3	Identification of text passages with a high density of tagged items	Automatic with Python script
Step 4	Analysis of high-density passages and identification of new stance markers	Manual analysis
Step 5	Further analysis of newly identified markers	Corpus-based analysis

Table 7 Twenty frequent and reliable stance markers in Early Modern English (Landert 2019: 177)

Verbs	*believe, doubt, know, perceive, seem, suppose, think*
Adjectives	*confident, evident, (un)likely, manifest, (im)possible, (im)probable, (un)sure*
Adverbs	*certainly, perhaps, plainly, surely, truly, verily*

clusters. Once found, these passages can then provide rich material for qualitative analysis. Thus, instead of analysing random or stratified subsets of individual instances from a corpus, extra work is invested in identifying passages that include such clusters, which are then submitted to qualitative analysis. The time-intensive manual investigation can be applied to those passages in a corpus that include most instances and which, as a consequence, may be especially relevant for understanding the phenomenon under investigation. In this way, more data can lead to richer observations without a linear increase of work time.

This idea has been applied to the study of epistemic stance in Early Modern English (Landert 2019). One of the aims of the research project was to identify stance expressions that had not been discussed in previous research. This included period-specific stance markers, lexical expressions that are only occasionally used as stance markers, and expressions that imply stance and whose stance meaning relies on an interpretation of the expression in context. In other words, the study adopted a function-to-form approach in which the full inventory of the forms was not known beforehand.

The method that was used to identify and analyse stance markers consists of several steps (see Table 6). In Step 1, a small set of frequent and reliable stance markers was identified. These items served as seed items that helped identify passages with a high density of stance markers. The candidate items for this set of markers were in part identified based on findings from previous research. The list was restricted to frequent lexical items and a manual analysis of a stratified sample of each lexical item was used to exclude items that were often used with meanings not related to stance. The final list of frequent and reliable stance markers consisted of twenty lexical items (see Table 7).

In Step 2, all instances of the twenty frequent and reliable stance markers were automatically tagged in four Early Modern English corpora (see Section 5.4 for a discussion of the four corpora). Following this, Step 3 involved the identification of passages that included many tagged items. Like Step 2, this was done in a fully automatic way, using a Python script. The study adopted a sliding-window approach, in which the number of tagged items was calculated in overlapping 300-word-passages (see Figure 4). The script then returned those passages with the highest number of tagged items. In Step 4, the passages with most tagged items were manually analysed and all stance markers in these passages were identified. The analysis showed that the passages that included many tagged items also contained other stance markers, including markers that had not been described so far. For instance, the verbs *collect* (meaning 'conclude') and *credit* (meaning 'believe') can both be used with epistemic meaning across all for Early Modern English corpora. Both verbs are not included in previous studies of epistemic stance. In Step 5, the final step of the analysis, the newly identified markers were studied in more detail in all four corpora, using established corpus-based methods (form-to-function approach).

The central step consists of the manual analysis of the high-density passages (Step 4). This detailed qualitative investigation can result in rich observations concerning the use of epistemic stance in Early Modern

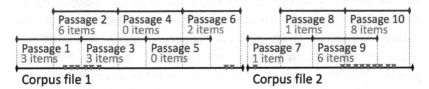

Figure 4 Illustration of the sliding-window approach to identify passages with a high density of tagged items

English. By retrieving passages that include a high density of known stance markers, the time-intensive manual analysis could be restricted to passages for which it was highly likely that they would result in relevant observations. In this way, the size of the combined corpora – about 6.6 million words – did not present an obstacle for the qualitative step in the analysis. On the contrary, more data means that it becomes more likely that passages with many stance markers are retrieved. By restricting the analysis to those passages with most tagged items, the number of passages that are analysed manually can remain manageable, even if more data is available overall.

6.5 Conclusion

In this section, we looked at ways in which studies that require a great deal of time-intensive qualitative analysis can still make use of the increasing size of corpus data that has become available. One key for resolving the tension between qualitative analysis and corpus size is the observation that many pragmatic features are not evenly distributed across texts. If we find ways of identifying text types, texts and passages within texts which include a high number of instances of the feature we are interested in, we can restrict the time-intensive qualitative analysis to these. Developing such methods will help improve the scalability of qualitative methods, so that they, too, can make the best use of the rich potential offered by large corpora.

7 Multimodality: Integrating Non-verbal Information

7.1 Introduction: Corpora beyond Language

When applied in corpus linguistics, multimodality broadly refers to the representation of more than one mode in a corpus. This may seem conceptually simple – understanding illustrations as well as written sentences as part of a book, or gaze and speech as part of a spoken interaction – but multimodality is in fact hard to define and operationalise for our context of corpus pragmatics. It is important to point out first of all that even monomodal corpora – consisting of systematically organised collections of written texts – are the product of a modal and/or medial transfer. Following the terminology employed, e.g. by Kress and Van Leeuwen (2001), Kaindl (2013) and Messerli (2020), corpus building may include an intramodal and intramedial transfer from written to written and from online text to online text. For instance, in the case of the *NOW* corpus, texts embedded in online environments such as news sites are recontextualised as online corpus texts read or searched on english-corpora.org.

Alternatively, as is the case for *CHILDES* in the TalkBank system, an inter-modal and intermedial transfer may take place from spoken to written and from face-to-face interaction to online text. While the *CHILDES* corpus consists primarily of transcripts, the data it represents consists of spoken interactions in some form of language learning setting.

Based on the transformation that happens in the process of corpus building, we may either be concerned with the representation of multimodality extant in the source – e.g. whether a corpus of newspaper articles contains and/or makes searchable the images that were included in the articles – or multimodality in representation – e.g. whether a corpus of spoken interaction contains the medium which it represents (spoken language) in addition to the medium in which it primarily represents the population (written text). As a result of this duality, a multimodal corpus may refer to a corpus that makes available modes beyond writing directly, e.g. by including digitised audio and video files (see, e.g., Allwood 2008), or to text collections that have annotation layers encoding other modes in writing, e.g. by transcribing hand gestures or emojis (see, e.g., Collins 2020).

Finally, to complicate things further, modes themselves are only partially defined ontologically in terms of the semiotic mechanisms they use to make meaning, and are also shaped by social contexts and practices (Kress 2010: 86–87), e.g. when it comes to deciding whether the materiality of the book and the font used in printing are a meaningful part of the text and the language of a novel.

Given these complexities and the fact that ever more settings of language use are represented in ever more different ways in linguistic corpora, it is clear that we cannot discuss all the possibilities and challenges of multimodal corpora in this section. Instead, we will limit ourselves to a subjective take on three questions:

(1) How are modes and media beyond writing included in corpora that are of interest to researchers in linguistic pragmatics?
(2) What examples in terms of corpora and studies are there at the time of writing?
(3) What challenges and opportunities lie ahead for multimodal corpus pragmatics?

7.2 Representing Modes and Media in Corpora

The composition of corpora always depends on the research they are intended for. Since pragmatics rests on the assumption that meaning depends on context, it is especially salient in the case of corpus pragmatic applications that decisions in the compilation of data collections for corpus research extend not only to type and number of included texts but beyond that to the representation of all semiotic codes involved in the meaning-making of texts as situated language use.

Prototypical questions are, for instance, how film and sound images can be included in corpora of television language (Bednarek 2015; Section 5) or audiovisual translation (AVT) (Soffritti 2018); how images in newspapers are incorporated in news media corpora (Landert 2014; Bednarek & Caple 2017); how emojis are represented in corpora of Facebook communication (Collins 2020) or viewer comments (Messerli & Locher 2021; see Section 7.6); or how features of orality in spoken interaction are included in respective corpora (Adolphs & Carter 2013). The answers for the analyst will be specific not only to each of the genres mentioned in this exemplary list but also to the pragmatic question for which the corpus is intended. What they all share, however, is the underlying problem of modelling acts of communication as they occur in their natural habitat within the world of the corpus, and how to reach a level of representation that allows the pragmatic researcher to analyse aspects of illocution and perlocution based on the corpus representation of the communicative acts.

7.3 Application 1: Memes

As an illustration, we will point to the small *Swiss Memes Corpus* (*SMC*) that was compiled for the study published in Dynel and Messerli (2020), which was interested in a cross-cultural comparison of humorous depictions of Switzerland in Swiss, Polish and international memes. The data collected for the corpus consisted of only a few hundred memes, collected from three different sites, with each meme considered a multimodal text. As one of the simpler examples of multimodality, each of these texts incorporates an arrangement of some form of image and written text, which together create meaning. For the study, the *SMC* was encoded as a simple table, consisting of the image of the meme, its written text encoded as plain text, and manual coding of themes into which the researchers categorised each text. For the purposes of the study, which rested mainly on the qualitative analysis of typical examples, the composition of the *SMC* allowed a selection of examples based on theme, and access to the multimodal – albeit decontextualised – representation of the meme including its visual components.

If we were to be interested, however, in a more representative picture of how Switzerland is positioned in these and similar memes – perhaps based on a larger corpus of memes –, a corpus that is only searchable based on meme captions and themes might be insufficient. The issue is that *SMC*, while including the visual imagery of each meme, does not make it searchable. It may be immediately recognisable, for instance, that many of the memes contain a Swiss flag, but that information is only usable for corpus analysis if the combination of encoding and corpus search interface allow access to it. For the different types of traditional corpora we have focused on up to this point in this Element, this means that we have to textually encode not only the captions but also aspects of the pictorial content of the memes.

7.4 Multimodality and Multimediality

If we stick to a traditional understanding of corpus linguistics, the main question of multimodality in corpora is thus not one of multimediality – how to include pictures or voice recordings together with written text – but of intersemiotic transfer: how can we encode more of the complex text and context of communicative acts in a way that is understandable by traditional corpus methods. Beyond traditional corpus designs, we may ask how we can expand corpus linguistic methods so they can systematically capture information that is not encoded in this way.

If multimodality is understood as a problem of encoding, multimodal corpora face similar problems to those of multimodal transcription (see, e.g., Baldry & Thibault 2006; Messerli 2020), with the additional pressure that transcription from anything other than written language to writing needs to be done in a fashion that is understandable not only to human readers, but also defined clearly and consistently enough that it can be included as a well-structured annotation (e.g. in the form of XML tags or stand-off) that makes it machine-readable.

If multimodality is multimediality, then the burden lies on the development of more sophisticated corpus architectures that can make machine-readable even what has not been manually made so. A case in point is the VIAN-DH project currently in development at the University of Zurich, which combines image recognition (e.g. of hand gestures) with conversation analytic and corpus methods to create a new research tool as well as a multimedial corpus of multimodal communication in video clips. Potentially, this makes it possible for a researcher to identify a particular hand gesture in the video or even use their laptop camera to record the gesture they perform themselves and search the corpus for occurrences of visually similar gestures.

As the brief sample of available multimodal corpora in Section 7.5 will show, such corpora are not yet widely available at the time of writing. The reason for this is the amount of expertise that is required for the compilation and maintenance of such corpora, but also the requirements for the infrastructure that hosts them. Instead, the multimodal corpora that exist employ modes beyond writing mostly to allow a more contextualised representation of language in use and/or make select multimodal aspects available by means of manual coding (see, e.g., the description of the *NMMC* in Adolphs & Carter 2013: 145–57).

7.5 Multimodal Corpora: A Sample of Currently Available Resources

To get an overview of available multimodal corpora, we can start with a cluster sample of those available on Europe's *CLARIN* infrastructure. Given the scarcity of such corpora, we will not limit ourselves to English language corpora here. Out of seventeen multimodal corpora on *CLARIN*, fifteen are on different genres of spoken language, whereas only two, the *Multimodal Corpus of Tourist Brochures Produced by the City of Helsinki, Finland (1967–2008)* and the *Hindi Visual Genome 1.0*, contain multimodal representations of written texts. The former is a textbook case of the encoding route described in Section 7.2 – apart from the brochures' text, it contains annotation for various aspects, including layout, typography and rhetorical structure.

The spoken multimodal corpora on *CLARIN* are dedicated to a range of different speech events or genres – from friendly conversations among people that know each other well in the *IFA Dialog Video corpus* to simulated job interviews in the *Hungarian Multimodal Corpus*. In terms of annotation, the corpora follow different standards, but often include some form of annotation of gaze and/or gestures. All corpora are small in size and there are very few resources present for any given language. If we assume a researcher in English corpus pragmatics, it is worth noting that only two corpora contain samples of spoken English including some multimodal aspects – the *Eye-tracking in Multimodal Interaction Corpus* and the *Bielefeld Speech and Gesture Alignment Corpus (SaGA)*.

Beyond *CLARIN*, notable multimodal corpora include corpora that allow for the searching of speech phenomena, which includes the more specialised *Buckeye Corpus of Conversational Speech* and *Switchboard Corpus*, the *Scottish Corpus of Texts & Speech (SCOTS)*, which includes texts and many aligned audio recordings, and the more general *BNC Audio*, which not only provides aligned audio clips for about half the spoken section of the *BNC*, but also includes phonemic transcription and makes searchable aspects of phonology such as syllable counts and stress patterns (see Hoffmann & Arndt-Lappe 2021). Other, similar examples of transcriptions with aligned audio include the new *London–Lund Corpus 2* (British English) and the *Santa Barbara Corpus of Spoken American English*.

Within the field of language acquisition, *CHILDES* is a large collection of corpora which contain transcripts of child language acquisition as their main text and sometimes accompanying audio and/or video files for contextualisation and illustration. Within studies of interpreting, Bernardini et al.

(2018) provide an overview of the multimodal aspects of the *European Parliament Interpreting Corpus* (*EPIC*), *EPICG* and *EPTIC* – three corpora of European Parliament plenary debates – and also incorporate a step-by-step guide of building a corpus that is not only multimodal, but also multilingual, thus requiring the alignment of both different modes and languages in order to allow the comparison of source and target languages in the context of interpreting (see Section 2.8).

Another important corpus pragmatic domain where multimodal corpora are central concerns the representation of sign languages. The volume edited by Fenlon and Hochgesang (2022) has recently mapped out in great detail the processes of building signed language corpora as well as their applications in existing and future research. Examples of multimodal sign language corpora mentioned are the early *Auslan Corpus*, with video recordings in the sign language Auslan, the *German Sign Language* (*DGS*) *Corpus* and the *British Sign Language* (*BSL*) *Corpus*. Interestingly, many of these corpora are not only available online but also provide detailed annotation guidelines, and in some cases templates for software like ELAN.

For the domain of text-image corpora, the *Lampeter Corpus of Early Modern English Tracts* (*LC*) is an example of a historical corpus that encodes visual aspects of the layout of historical tracts. In the context of computer-mediated communication, Christiansen et al. (2020) propose to employ what they term Visual Constituent Analysis (VCA) in the building of corpora containing, in particular, posts to social media. The importance of visual non-verbal components of online posts such as tweets cannot be overstated, and the simple example of searching tweets for names like 'Clinton' or 'Trump' shows that while maybe half the tweets about Donald Trump and Hillary Clinton in a given corpus can be found this way, the other half refers to either of the two US American politicians by means of a picture but without textual reference (Christiansen et al. 2020, working on the first iteration of the *Twitter Internet Research Agency Repository*). The way out proposed as part of VCA is to make use of commercially available automatic image annotation, e.g. Google Cloud Vision, to not only make texts in images readable by means of OCR, but also to enrich them with labels including named entities, recognised objects or parts of human bodies and faces, and even intertextual aspects that link individual posts to, for instance, other people and institutions. This is one way of encoding multimodality in monomodal written text, while avoiding the often prohibitive laboriousness of entirely manual coding (see Section 6).

While Christiansen et al.'s (2020) project again points to ways of addressing multimodality that take us beyond conventional corpus pragmatics, Section 7.6

illustrates the questions and challenges of multimodality based on a more traditional corpus-based study design.

7.6 Application 2: Humour Support in Viewer Comments

As part of a project dedicated to communicative practices in English fansub-titles and viewer comments to Korean TV drama, Messerli and Locher (2021) address what they have termed humour support indicators (HCIs) in a corpus of textual comments that fans write while streaming episodes on viki.com. The communicative setting modeled by the corpus consists of a viewer connecting to the streaming site through a web browser or a dedicated app on a phone, laptop or TV. Within the active window or app, there is video and audio, fansubtitles in the conventional position central at the bottom, and the comments themselves superimposed on the picture or in a separate window to its side. Finally, the comments themselves not only contain written text but also make abundant use of emojis.

The corpus design for the project consists of two corpora, one for the comments and one for the English fansubtitles. The two corpora are aligned based on the shared time code, relative to the episode streams, and the same time codes allow access to the entirety of semiotic modes on the streaming platform itself. The corpus of comments (*KTACC*) is designed as a monomodal collection, but contains unicode characters for the emojis, so that they, too, are searchable like words. For the purposes of the study, this makes it possible, for instance, to identify collocations of emojis and laugh particles – say 'hahaha' together with 😂 – or simple frequency searches to identify what emoji is employed by users most often. However, when the researchers wanted to identify icons that have a humorous meaning, manual identification of individual emojis was necessary, a step akin to identifying IFIDs for humour support.

Due to the frequency of emojis, this representation of the multimodality is as crucial for the understanding of humour support in viewer comments as the pictorial content in tweets highlighted by Christiansen et al. (2020). While this aspect was thus incorporated into *KTACC*, and the interplay between comments and subtitles was approached by means of a time-aligned corpus design, perhaps equally crucial relationships between the comments, subtitles and streamed videos are a blind spot for the corpus. Accordingly, most insights gained so far into these relationships have been due to exhaustive manual coding of samples (Locher 2020; Locher & Messerli 2020).

7.7 Conclusion

The corpus pragmatic community has, at the time of writing, only just begun to find ways of incorporating more of the multimodality that is crucial to any genre of situated language use into corpus designs. While corpora such as those outlined in Section 7.5 may include multimediality, i.e. data beyond written language, and provide access to multimodality by means of (en)coding non-linguistic semiotic modes, for the time being corpora are strictly speaking almost universally monomodal representations of multimodal actions. This does in no way undermine the value of corpus pragmatic research – a model of reality that includes a reduction of complexity is arguably at the basis of all research – but it requires at least awareness that such a reduction has taken place, and ideally the exploration of new ways to incorporate other modes into new corpus designs, and other methods into corpus-based study designs.

The avenues we have outlined here constitute three main areas:

(1) mixed-method studies that combine horizontal reading with corpus analyses;
(2) studies that encode visual or audio information in plain text – typically manually by trained coders, but sometimes automatically, e.g. through machine-learning-based image recognition tools;
(3) and potentially new corpus search interfaces that dynamically adapt to researchers' needs through processes like active learning, thus opening up new possibilities for the identification of communicative patterns in multimodal text.

Given recent developments in all three areas, we expect that multimodal corpus pragmatic research will gain a lot of importance in the next years and will likely lead to exciting new insights into language use in context.

8 Open Issues and Outlook

At the beginning of this Element, we argued that the advantages of doing corpus pragmatics can be found in pattern finding, systematicity, generalisation, reproducibility and transparency (Section 1.6), and throughout this Element we attempted to illustrate these key features. To conclude, the following subsections give a brief summary of the challenges and opportunities of corpus pragmatics that we discussed throughout the various sections of this Element. We include suggestions of how to engage with corpus pragmatics and we end with a brief outlook.

8.1 Corpus Methods for Function-to-Form Approaches

One of the areas in which we see great potential for future research is the development of corpus methods that are specifically tailored towards the study of pragmatic functions. Since the earliest days of corpus linguistics, researchers have used corpora to study pragmatic phenomena. Nevertheless, many of the tools that are most commonly used to search and analyse corpus data have been developed for the study of grammar and lexicon. This has led to an abundance of options to study forms in corpora: e.g. concordances, collocations, n-grams and keywords. All these options can be used in form-to-function approaches of corpus pragmatics. In contrast, the options for function-to-form approaches are much scarcer.

In this Element, we have pointed out several ways in which corpora can be used for function-to-form approaches. In Section 4, we presented corpus-assisted approaches, in which researchers analyse small self-compiled datasets in a systematic manner and where corpus tools and qualitative data analysis software make it possible to quantify observations across different sections of the data. In Section 3, we discussed data-driven approaches, where differences in pragmatic functions – such as persuasion – are identified through aspects that are an integral part of the original data – such as user annotations. And in Section 6, we presented approaches in which well-known aspects of the typical distribution of pragmatic functions were used as a starting point for research: the placement of pragmatic functions in specific texts and parts of texts, and the tendency of pragmatic functions to cluster together. We think that exploring these and similar new methods that build closely on the typical characteristics of pragmatic functions holds a great deal of potential for the further development of corpus pragmatics.

8.2 Combining Quantitative and Qualitative Methods

Corpus approaches are predestined for quantification. Corpora include well-defined datasets that make it possible to identify linguistic features in a systematic manner. By comparing the frequency of such observations across different sections of data, we can draw conclusions about the distribution of such features in language use more generally. Thus, quantification is an integral part of corpus pragmatic methods. However, it would be problematic to reduce corpus pragmatics – or corpus linguistics in general – to quantification (see also Egbert et al. 2020: ch. 7). Qualitative analysis is equally crucial. In order to understand pragmatic functions, we need to engage in interpretations of language use in context, as we discussed in Section 1. This means that both quantitative and qualitative steps are involved in corpus pragmatics.

Quantitative and qualitative methods can be combined in various ways. We may start with detailed manual analysis that focuses on the identification of patterns, which is then applied to the overall corpus (see Section 4). Alternatively, we can take as our starting point the overall frequency distribution of linguistic characteristics across different sets of data, and then study these characteristics in more detail. We discussed an example of such an approach in Section 3. As a third option, Section 6 discussed studies that use previous knowledge about pragmatics as a starting point to retrieve passages that can provide rich insight into the realisation of a pragmatic function when analysed qualitatively. The resulting observations can then be used for further quantitative and qualitative steps in the analysis.

8.3 Opportunities and Challenges of New Corpus Resources

Linguistic corpora have undergone a great deal of diversification since the early days of corpus linguistics. In Section 2, we emphasised this point by illustrating some of the characteristics that distinguish corpora from each other. The characteristics we discuss there are not mutually exclusive, and they can combine in any number of ways to create unique new corpus resources. Some of these new kinds of corpora hold special potential for pragmatic research. For instance, pragmatically annotated corpora make it possible to search for pragmatic functions and to take into account factors that affect the realisation of pragmatic features. Another example is multimodal corpora, which we discussed in detail in Section 7. By including sound, images and videos, such corpora allow researchers to study language use in its multimodal context. Finally, the rapid advances in computational linguistics create the potential for new ways of automatic and semi-automatic annotation, including annotation of pragmatic phenomena, and are likely to offer new approaches to the study of pragmatic phenomena in corpora.

As corpora become more diverse in structure and composition, new challenges for the compatibility and comparability of corpus resources will present themselves (see Section 5). Developing tools that support smooth and reliable working across different corpora without sacrificing metainformation and annotation will be crucial. Such tools should be open access in order to make it possible for researchers to control and adjust how corpus data is treated. Projects such as *AntConc*, *LancsBox* and *NoSketch Engine* are very valuable in this respect. As new kinds of corpus resources are being developed, it will be important to pay attention to the specific needs of pragmatic studies. These needs include, for instance, the option of accessing context beyond just a few words to the left and right of a search term. Equally crucial is the availability of transparent metainformation on the origin of the data that is included in a corpus, as well as any factors that may influence how pragmatic features are realised.

8.4 Data Awareness

Another issue we want to highlight is that corpus pragmaticists, like all corpus linguists in general, have a duty to inform themselves about the corpus they are working with (see Egbert et al. 2020: ch. 2). They need to know how the compilation of the corpus went about and what principles guided the sampling of texts. In Section 5, on comparability, we talked about this issue in relation to working with different corpora in combination. Even when working with just one corpus, it is equally important that users of a corpus know about what kind of data they are working with. If you are working with your own self-compiled data, you are in control and know what is 'in' the corpus. If you work with corpora provided by others, it is your duty as a scholar to inform yourself about its compilation so that you can better assess how this corpus is suitable for your research needs. Such information is usually accessible in publications about a corpus or online information that accompanies the corpus, although the amount of quality of information that is available varies a great deal. Especially for large corpora that integrate unmonitored data – often from online sources that are freely available – reliable information about the origin and context of the corpus data is often not provided to a sufficient extent.

For researchers compiling their own corpora, there are additional require-ments with respect to the ethics of data collection. In Section 3.3, we have given some pointers to sources that help corpus pragmatics scholars in their attempt to make decisions concerning ethical conduct and heeding copyright concerns when compiling a corpus. Just like in any data collection, scholars in corpus pragmatics too need to be informed about ethics when using an existing corpus and take ethics considerations into account when compiling corpora from scratch. Especially for big corpora, incorporating ethics consid-erations remains a challenge and viable solutions have to be found for each corpus independently.

8.5 Where to Start?

This Element has presented a brief summary of many different approaches. Consulting the references mentioned in the respective section is certainly a good starting point to begin a research project on any of them. For further practical examples and guidance, Rühlemann (2019) presents an introduction to different areas of corpus pragmatic research based on the *BNC*. For a more detailed discussion of theoretical background, Aijmer and Rühlemann's (2014) handbook *Corpus Pragmatics* can be consulted, which provides a rich overview of relevant concepts and previous research.

As we emphasised throughout the Element, any corpus pragmatic study should start by engaging closely with the corpus, the data it includes and the principles according to which it was compiled. The list of corpora in Appendix A includes a large range of different corpora which have been used for pragmatic research. Any of these can be explored for additional aspects of pragmatics. Appendix B includes further tools that can be applied in corpus pragmatic studies, for instance when working with self-compiled corpora.

8.6 Creativity and Dynamics of the Field and Outlook

Corpus linguistics has been at the forefront of digital research in the humanities for more than forty years, and corpus pragmatics has enriched it through dynamic and creative contributions. We cannot stress enough that this field is dynamic in itself and calls for dynamic solutions at the same time. While we keep developing new ways of approaching pragmatic research challenges with existing corpora, new technological possibilities are being developed and are drawn on in order to tackle our research questions. These technical affordances are constantly evolving so that any new project design will face questions regarding whether to work with existing corpora (that might not be ideal in their composition or in the way one can work with them) or build new corpora (and engaging in a labour-intensive process of corpus creation and deciding how to ensure compatibility and comparability with existing resources). Establishing best practices and guidelines will remain crucial for as long as new corpora and tools are becoming available – which we are confident will be the case for the foreseeable future.

Appendix A: Corpora

The following list presents all corpora mentioned in the Element, including information on where to access them and/or find additional information about them.

ARCHER. A Representative Corpus of Historical English Registers. ARCHER Consortium. (1993–). www.projects.alc.manchester.ac.uk/archer/.

The Auslan Corpus. Johnston, Trevor A. et al. (2008–). https://auslan.org.au.

BASE. British Academic Spoken English Corpus. Thompson, Paul & Nesi, Hilary. (2001). The British Academic Spoken English (BASE) Corpus Project. *Language Teaching Research* 5(3), 263–4. www.sketchengine.eu/british-academic-spoken-english-corpus/.

BBC. Birmingham Blog Corpus. (2010). Compiled by the Research and Development Unit for English Studies at Birmingham City University. www.webcorp.org.uk/blogs.

BNC1994. British National Corpus. BNC Consortium. (1991–). www.natcorp.ox.ac.uk/.

BNC2014. British National Corpus 2014. http://corpora.lancs.ac.uk/bnc2014/.

BNC Audio. Audio part of the British National Corpus. See BNC1994.

Brexit Corpus. SENSEI-EU. University of Trento, Websays.com & Aix-Marseille University. (2016). www.sense-eu.info/, www.sketchengine.eu/news/brexit-corpus-referendum/.

Brown Corpus. Kučera, Henry & Francis, W. Nelson. (1964/1979). http://icame.uib.no/brown/bcm.html.

BSL. British Sign Language Corpus. (2008–11). Cormier, Kearsy, Schembri, Adam, Fenlon, Jordan, et al. https://bslcorpusproject.org.

Buckeye Corpus of Conversational Speech. The Ohio State University. (2007, 2nd release). https://buckeyecorpus.osu.edu/.

CANBEC. Cambridge and Nottingham Business English Corpus. University of Nottingham, UK & Cambridge University Press. (2003). Not publicly available.

CED. Corpus of English Dialogues 1560–1760. Kytö, Merja & Culpeper, Jonathan. (2006). Oxford Text Archive, http://hdl.handle.net/20.500.12024/2507.

CEEM. Corpus of Early English Medical Writing. Taavitsainen, Irma, Pahta, Päivi & Mäkinen, Martti. (1995–2019).

MEMT. Middle English Medical Texts 1375 – 1500. (2005). John Benjamins.

EMEMT. Early Modern English Medical Texts 1500–1700. (2010). John Benjamins.

LMEMT. Late Modern English Medical Texts 1700–1800. (2019). John Benjamins.

CHELAR. Corpus of Historical English Law Reports 1535–1999. Rodríguez-Puente, Paula, Fanego, Teresa, José López-Couso, María, Méndez-Naya, Belén & Núñez-Pertejo, Paloma. (2016). www.usc-vlcg.es/CHELAR.htm.

CHILDES. Child Language Data Exchange System. MacWhinney, Brian. (1984). https://childes.talkbank.org/.

CLMET. The Corpus of Late Modern English Texts, version 3.0. Diller, Hans-Jürgen, De Smet, Hendrik & Tyrkkö, Jukka. (2011). https://perswww.kuleu ven.be/~u0044428/clmet3_0.htm.

COCA. The Corpus of Contemporary American English. Davies, Mark. (2008–). www.english-corpora.org/coca/.

COHA. The Corpus of Historical American English. Davies, M. (2010). www.english-corpora.org/coha/.

Corpus of Czech Students' Spoken English. Šárka Ježková, Univerzita Pardubice. (2015). https://bit.ly/3iPw9fT.

DGS. Corpus of German Sign Language. (2009–23). Hanke, Thomas, Herrmann, Annika, Rathmann, Christian et al. www.sign-lang.uni-hamburg.de/.

DOE. Dictionary of Old English Corpus. (1981/2009). www.doe.utoronto.ca.

EEBO. Early English Books Online. https://proquest.libguides.com/eebopqp.

EMEMT. See CEEM.

EPIC. European Parliament Interpreting Corpus. (2011). https://cris.unibo .it/handle/11585/132580.

EUROPARL. European Parliament Proceedings Parallel Corpus 1996–2011. www.statmt.org/europarl/.

Eye-tracking in Multimodal Interaction Corpus. Holler, Judith & Kendrick, Kobin. (2013–14). MPI for Psycholinguistics Archive. https://bit.ly/ 3VLAuzi.

GLBCC. Giessen–Long Beach Chaplin Corpus. Jucker, Andreas H., Müller, Simone & Smith, Sara. (2006). Oxford Text Archive. http://hdl.handle.net/ 20.500.12024/2506.

GloWbE. Corpus of Global Web-Based English. Davies, Mark. (2013). www.english-corpora.org/glowbe/.

HC. Helsinki Corpus of English Texts. (1991). Oxford Text Archive, http://hdl. handle.net/20.500.12024/1477. (2011). https://helsinkicorpus.arts.gla.ac .uk/display.py?what=index.

Hindi Visual Genome 1.0. Parida, Shantipriya, Bojar, Ondrej & Dash, Satya Ranjan. (2019). https://ufal.mff.cuni.cz/hindi-visual-genome.

Hungarian Multimodal Corpus. (2013). https://hdl.handle.net/1839/00-0000-0000-001A-E17C-1.

ICE. International Corpus of English. (1990–). www.ice-corpora.uzh.ch/en.html.

ICLE. International Corpus of Learner English. Granger, Sylviane. (2002/2009). https://uclouvain.be/en/research-institutes/ilc/cecl/icle.html.

IFA Dialog Video corpus. Nederlandse Taal Unie. (2007). www.fon.hum.uva.nl/IFA-SpokenLanguageCorpora/IFADVcorpus/.

KTACC. Korean television drama Time-Aligned Comments Corpus. Locher, Miriam & Messerli, Thomas. Not publicly available.

LC. The Lampeter Corpus of Early Modern English Tracts. Schmid, Josef, Claridge, Claudia & Siemund, Rainer. (1999). http://korpus.uib.no/icame/manuals/LAMPETER/LAMPHOME.HTM.

LINDSEI. Louvain International Database of Spoken English Interlanguage. Gilquin, Gaëtanelle, De Cock, Sylvie & Granger, Sylviane. (2010). https://bit.ly/3Bmhr6t.

LLC. London-Lund Corpus of Spoken English. (1990). Svartvik, Jan. Oxford Text Archive. http://hdl.handle.net/20.500.12024/0168.

LLC2. London–Lund Corpus 2. (in progress). https://projekt.ht.lu.se/llc2.

LMEMT. See CEEM.

LOB. Lancaster–Oslo/Bergen Corpus. (1978). Leech, Geoffrey, Johansson, Stig & Hofland, Knut. http://korpus.uib.no/icame/manuals/LOB/INDEX.HTM.

Longman Corpus of Spoken and Written English. www.pearsonlongman.com/dictionaries/corpus/index.html.

MEMT. See CEEM.

MICASE. The Michigan Corpus of Academic Spoken English. Simpson, R. C., Briggs, S. L., Ovens, J. & Swales, J. M. (2002). Ann Arbor, MI: The Regents of the University of Michigan. https://quod.lib.umich.edu/m/micase/.

Movie Corpus. Davies, Mark. (2019). www.english-corpora.org/movies/.

Multimodal Corpus of Tourist Brochures Produced by the City of Helsinki, Finland (1967–2008). Hippala, Tuomo. (2015). http://urn.fi/urn:nbn:fi:lb-201411281.

NMMC. Nottingham Multimodal Corpus. See Adolphs & Carter (2013) for further information.

NOW. The Corpus of News on the Web. Davies, Mark. (2016–). www.english-corpora.org/now/.

OBC. Old Bailey Corpus 2.0. Huber, Magnus, Nissel, Magnus & Puga, Karin. (2016). hdl:11858/00-246 C-0000-0023-8CFB-2 / www1.uni-giessen.de/oldbaileycorpus/. www.oldbaileyonline.org/static/Project.jsp.

PCEEC. Parsed Corpus of Early English Correspondence. CEEC Project Team. (2006). Oxford Text Archive. http://hdl.handle.net/20.500.12024/2510.

SaGA. Bielefeld Speech and Gesture Alignment Corpus. www.phonetik.uni-muenchen.de/Bas/BasSaGAeng.html.

SBC. Santa Barbara Corpus of Spoken American English. Du Bois, John W., Chafe, Wallace L., Meyer, Charles, et al. (2000–2005). www.linguistics.ucsb.edu/research/santa-barbara-corpus.

SCOTS. Scottish Corpus of Texts & Speech. Kay, Christian, Thompson, Henry, Corbett, John, et al. (2002–4). www.scottishcorpus.ac.uk/.

SMC. Swiss Memes Corpus. Dynel, Marta & Messerli, Thomas. Not publicly available.

SOAP. Corpus of American Soap Operas. Davies, Mark. (2011-). www.english-corpora.org/soap/.

SPC. Sociopragmatic Corpus; part of CED. Corpus of English Dialogues 1500–1700. Not publicly available.

SPICE-Ireland Corpus. Kirk, John M. & Kallen, Jeffrey L. (2011). https://johnmkirk.etinu.net/cgi-bin/generic?instanceID=11.

Switchboard Corpus. Godfrey, John J. & Holliman, Edward. (1992–7). https://catalog.ldc.upenn.edu/LDC97S62.

SydTV. Sydney Corpus of Television Dialogue. Bednarek, Monika. (2020). https://cqpw-prod.vip.sydney.edu.au/CQPweb/.

TV Corpus. Davies, Mark. (2019). www.english-corpora.org/tv/.

Twitter Internet Research Agency Repository (First Iteration). (2018). https://archive.org/details/twitter-ira.

VOICE. Vienna-Oxford International Corpus of English 3.0 online. (2021). https://voice.acdh.oeaw.ac.at/.

Appendix B: Corpus Tools and Additional Resources

The following list provides an overview of corpus linguistic tools and platforms that were mentioned throughout the Element.

AntConc. www.laurenceanthony.net/software/antconc/.

ATLAS.ti. https://atlasti.com/.

BNClab. http://corpora.lancs.ac.uk/bnclab/search.

CATMA. Computer Assisted Text Markup and Analysis. https://catma.de/.

CLARIN. Common Language Resources and Technology Infrastructure. www.clarin.eu/.

CoRD. Corpus Resource Database. https://varieng.helsinki.fi/CoRD/index.html.

CQPweb. Web-based graphical user interface for CWB. https://cwb.source forge.io/cqpweb.php.

CWB. IMS Open Corpus Workbench. https://cwb.sourceforge.io/.

DART. Dialogue Annotation and Research Tool. See Weisser (2014).

Google Ngram Viewer. https://books.google.com/ngrams.

koRpus. Text analysis package for R. https://cran.r-project.org/web/packages/koRpus/index.html.

LancsBox. Lancaster University Corpus Toolbox. http://corpora.lancs.ac.uk/lancsbox/.

MAXQDA. www.maxqda.de/.

NLTK. Natural Language Toolkit. www.nltk.org/.

NoSketch Engine. https://nlp.fi.muni.cz/trac/noske.

NVivo. https://bit.ly/3HueNzk.

OTA. Oxford Text Archive. https://ota.bodleian.ox.ac.uk/repository/xmlui/.

Oxygen XML Editor. www.oxygenxml.com/.

polmineR. R-based package for corpus analysis using the CWB. https://cran.r-project.org/web/packages/polmineR/index.html.

quanteda. Quantitative Analysis of Textual Data. https://quanteda.io/.

Sketch Engine. www.sketchengine.eu/.

spaCy. Python library for natural language processing. https://spacy.io/.

SPSS. IBM SPSS Statistics Platform. www.ibm.com/ch-de/products/spss-statistics.

TXM. Open source text analysis software. https://txm.gitpages.huma-num.fr/textometrie/en/index.html.

Wordsmith Tools. www.lexically.net/wordsmith/.

References

Adolphs, Svenja. (2008). *Corpus and Context: Investigating Pragmatic Functions in Spoken Discourse*. Amsterdam: John Benjamins.

Adolphs, Svenja & Carter, Ronald. (2013). *Spoken Corpus Linguistics: From Monomodal to Multimodal*. New York: Routledge.

Aijmer, Karin. (1997). *I think* – An English modal particle. In Swan, Toril & Westvik, Olaf Jansen, eds., *Modality in Germanic Languages: Historical and Comparative Perspectives*. Berlin: Mouton de Gruyter, pp. 1–47.

Aijmer, Karin. (2002). *English Discourse Particles: Evidence from a Corpus*. Amsterdam: John Benjamins.

Aijmer, Karin. (2008). At the interface between grammar and discourse: A corpus-based study of some pragmatic markers. In Romero-Trillo, Jesús, ed., *Pragmatics and Corpus Linguistics: A Mutualistic Entente*. Berlin: De Gruyter Mouton, pp. 11–36.

Aijmer, Karin. (2013). *Understanding Pragmatic Markers: A Variational Pragmatic Approach*. Edinburgh: Edinburgh University Press.

Aijmer, Karin & Rühlemann, Christoph, eds. (2014). *Corpus Pragmatics: A Handbook*. Cambridge: Cambridge University Press.

Allwood, Jens. (2008). Multimodal Corpora. In Lüdeling, Anke & Kytö, Merja, eds., *Corpus Linguistics: An International Handbook* (Vol. 1). Berlin: De Gruyter Mouton, pp. 207–25.

Andersen, Gisle. (2011). Corpus-based pragmatics I: Qualitative studies. In Bublitz, Wolfram & Norrick, Neal R., eds., *Foundations of Pragmatics* (Handbook of Pragmatics Series 1). Berlin: Walter de Gruyter, pp. 587–627.

Archer, Dawn. (2005). *Questions and Answers in the English Courtroom (1640–1760)* (Pragmatics & Beyond New Series 135). Amsterdam: John Benjamins.

Archer, Dawn & Gillings, Matthew. (2020). Depictions of deception: A corpus-based analysis of five Shakespearean characters. *Language and Literature* 29(3), 1–29. https://doi.org/10.1177/0963947020949439.

Baker, Paul. (2006). *Using Corpora in Discourse Analysis* (Continuum Discourse Series). London: Continuum.

Baldry, Anthony, & Thibault, Paul J. (2006). *Multimodal Transcription and Text Analysis*. London: Equinox.

Bayley, Paul & Williams, Geoffrey, eds. (2012). *European Identity: What the Media Say*. Oxford: Oxford University Press.

Bednarek, Monika. (2015). Corpus-assisted multimodal discourse analysis of television and film narratives. In Baker, Paul & McEnery, Tony, eds., *Corpora and Discourse Studies*. Basingstoke: Palgrave Macmillan, pp. 63–87.

Bednarek, Monika. (2018). *Language and Television Series: A Linguistic Approach to TV Dialogue* (Cambridge Applied Linguistics). Cambridge: Cambridge University Press.

Bednarek, Monika, & Caple, Helen. (2017). *The Discourse of News Values*. Oxford: Oxford University Press.

Bednarek, Monika, Veirano Pinto, Marcia & Werner, Valentin. (2021). Corpus approaches to telecinematic language: Introduction. *International Journal of Corpus Linguistics* 26(1), 1–9.

Beeching, Kate. (2016). *Pragmatic Markers in British English: Meaning in Social Interaction*. Cambridge: Cambridge University Press.

Bernardini, Silvia, Ferraresi, Adriano, Russo, Marachiara, Collard, Camille & Defrancq, Bart. (2018). Building interpreting and intermodal corpora: A how-to for a formidable task. In Russo, Mariachiara, Bendazzoli, Claudio & Defrancq, Bart, eds., *Making Way in Corpus-Based Interpreting Studies*. Singapore: Springer, pp. 21–42.

Biber, Douglas. (1988). *Variation across Speech and Writing*. Cambridge: Cambridge University Press.

Biber, Douglas. (1993). Representativeness in corpus design. *Literary and Linguistic Computing* 8(4), 243–257.

Blaette, Andreas. (2020). *polmineR: Verbs and Nouns for Corpus Analysis*. https://doi.org/10.5281/zenodo.4042093, R package version 0.8.2.

Brinton, Laurel J. (2012). Historical pragmatics and corpus linguistics: Problems and strategies. In Kytö, Merja, ed., *English Corpus Linguistics: Crossing Paths*. Amsterdam: Rodopi, pp. 101–31.

Burr, Vivien. (1995). *An Introduction to Social Constructionism*. London: Routledge.

Butler, Christopher S. (2008). The subjectivity of *basically* in British English: A corpus-based study. In Romero-Trillo, Jesús, ed., *Pragmatics and Corpus Linguistics: A Mutualistic Entente*. Berlin: Mouton de Gruyter, pp. 37–63.

Buysse, Lieven. (2012). *So* as a multifunctional discourse marker in native and learner speech. *Journal of Pragmatics* 44(13), 1764–82.

Buysse, Lieven. (2017). The pragmatic marker *you know* in learner English. *Journal of Pragmatics* 121, 40–57.

Buysse, Lieven. (2020). "It was a bit stressy as well actually": The pragmatic markers *actually* and *in fact* in spoken learner English. *Journal of Pragmatics* 156, 28–40.

Cartoni, Bruno, Zufferey, Sandrine & Meyer, Thomas. (2013). Using the Europarl corpus for cross-linguistic research. *Belgian Journal of Linguistics* 27(1), 23–42.

Christiansen, Alex, Dance, William & Wild, Alexander. (2020). Constructing corpora from images and text: An introduction to Visual Constituent Analysis. In Rüdiger, Sofia & Dayter, Daria, eds., *Corpus Approaches to Social Media*. Amsterdam: John Benjamins, pp. 149–74.

Collins, Luke. (2020). Working with images and emoji in the Dukki Facebook Corpus. In Rüdiger, Sofia & Dayter, Daria, eds., *Corpus Approaches to Social Media*. Amsterdam: John Benjamins, pp. 175–96.

Culpeper, Jonathan & Archer, Dawn. (2008). Requests and directness in Early Modern English trial proceedings and play texts, 1640–1760. In Jucker, Andreas H. & Taavitsainen, Irma, eds., *Speech Acts in the History of English* (Pragmatics & Beyond New Series 176). Amsterdam: John Benjamins, pp. 45–84.

Culpeper, Jonathan & Kytö, Merja. (2010). *Early Modern English Dialogues: Spoken Interaction as Writing*. Cambridge: Cambridge University Press.

Dayter, Daria. (2016). *Discursive Self in Microblogging: Speech Acts, Stories and Self-Praise*. Amsterdam: John Benjamins.

Dayter, Daria. (2018). Self-praise online and offline: The hallmark speech act of social media? *Internet Pragmatics* 1(1), 184–203.

Dayter, Daria. (2021). Dealing with interactionally risky speech acts in simultaneous interpreting: The case of self-praise. *Journal of Pragmatics* 174, 28–42.

Dayter, Daria, & Messerli, Thomas C. (2022). Persuasive language and features of formality on the r/ChangeMyView subreddit. *Internet Pragmatics* 5(1), 165–95. https://doi.org/10.1075/ip.00072.day.

Dayter, Daria & Rüdiger, Sofia. (2022). *The Language of Pick-Up Artists: Online Discourses of the Seduction Industry*. London: Routledge.

DeCapua, Andrea, & Dunham, Joan Findlay. (2012). 'It wouldn't hurt if you had your child evaluated': Advice to mothers in responses to vignettes from a US teaching context. In Limberg, Holger & Locher, Miriam A., eds., *Advice in Discourse*. Amsterdam: John Benjamins, pp. 73–96.

Deutschmann, Mats. (2003). *Apologising in British English* (Skrifter Från Moderna Språk 10). Umeå: Institutionen för moderna språk, Umeå University.

Doval, Irene & Sánchez Nieto, Teresa. (2019). *Parallel Corpora for Contrastive and Translation Studies*. Amsterdam: John Benjamins.

Dynel, Marta, & Messerli, Thomas C. (2020). On a cross-cultural memescape: Switzerland through nation memes from within and from the outside. *Contrastive Pragmatics* 1(2), 1–32.

Egbert, Jesse, Larsson, Tove & Biber, Douglas. (2020). *Doing Linguistics with a Corpus. Methodological Considerations for the Everyday User* (Elements in Corpus Linguistics). Cambridge: Cambridge University Press.

Evert, Stefan & Hardie, Andrew. (2011). Twenty-first century corpus workbench: Updating a query architecture for the new millennium. *Proceedings of the Corpus Linguistics 2011 Conference*, University of Birmingham, UK.

Fenlon, Jordan, & Hochgesang, Julie A. (eds.) (2022). *Signed Language Corpora*. Washington, DC: Gallaudet University Press.

Franzke, Aline, Bechmann, Anja, Zimmer, Michael, Ess, Charles & the Association of Internet Researchers. (2020). Internet Research: Ethical Guidelines 3.0. https://aoir.org/reports/ethics3.pdf.

Garcés-Conejos Blitvich, Pilar & Sifianou, Maria. (2019). Im/politeness and discursive pragmatics. *Journal of Pragmatics* 145, 91–101.

Gast, Volker. (2015). On the use of translation corpora in contrastive linguistics. *Languages in Contrast* 15(1), 4–33.

Gilquin, Gaëtanelle. (2008). Hesitation markers among EFL learners: Pragmatic deficiency or difference? In Romero-Trillo, Jesús, ed., *Pragmatics and Corpus Linguistics: A Mutualistic Entente*. Berlin: Mouton de Gruyter, pp. 119–49.

Gray, Bethany, Biber, Douglas & Hiltunen, Turo. (2011). The expression of stance in early (1665–1712) publications of the *Philosophical Transactions* and other contemporary medical prose: Innovations in a pioneering discourse. In Taavitsainen, Irma & Pahta, Päivi, eds., *Medical Writing in Early Modern English* (Studies in English Language). Cambridge: Cambridge University Press, pp. 221–57.

Guest, Greg, MacQueen, Kathleen M. & Namey, Emily E. (2012). *Applied Thematic Analysis*. Los Angeles, CA: SAGE Publications.

Harrison, Simon, Todd, Zazie & Lawton, Rebecca. (2008). Talk about terrorism and the media: Communicating with the conduit metaphor. *Communication, Culture and Critique* 1(4), 378–95.

Haugh, Michael. (2018). Corpus-based metapragmatics. In Jucker, Andreas H., Schneider, Klaus P. & Bublitz, Wolfram, eds., *Methods in Pragmatics* (Handbooks of Pragmatics 10). Berlin: De Gruyter Mouton, pp. 587–618.

Heinrich, Philipp & Schäfer, Fabian. (2018). Extending corpus-based discourse analysis for exploring Japanese social media. In Tono, Yukio & Isahara, Hitoshi, eds., *Proceedings of 4th Asia Pacific Corpus Linguistics Conference (APCLC2018)*, pp. 135–40.

Hilbert, Michaela & Krug, Manfred. (2010). The compilation of ICE Malta: State of the art and challenges along the way. *ICAME Journal* 34, 54–63.

Hoffmann, Sebastian, & Arndt-Lappe, Sabine. (2021). Better data for more researchers: Using the audio features of BNCweb. *ICAME Journal* 45(1), 125–54. https://doi.org/10.2478/icame-2021-0004.

Huschová, Petra. (2021). Modalized speech acts in a spoken learner corpus: The case of *can* and *could*. *Topics in Linguistics*, 22(1), 27–37. https://doi.org/10.2478/topling-2021-0003.

Ifukor, Presley. (2010). "Elections" or "selections"? Blogging and twittering the Nigerian 2007 general elections. *Bulletin of Science, Technology & Society* 30(6), 398–414.

Jacobs, Andreas & Jucker, Andreas H. (1995). The historical perspective in pragmatics. In Jucker, Andreas H., ed., *Historical Pragmatics. Pragmatic Developments in the History of English* (Pragmatics and Beyond New Series 35). Amsterdam: John Benjamins, pp. 3–33.

Jucker, Andreas H. (2004). Gutenberg und das Internet. Der Einfluss von Informationsmedien auf Sprache und Sprachwissenschaft. *Networx 40*. www.mediensprache.net/de/networx/docs/networx-40.aspx.

Jucker, Andreas H. (2013). Corpus Pragmatics. In Östman, Jan-Ola & Verschueren, Jef, eds., *Handbook of Pragmatics*. Amsterdam: John Benjamins, pp. 1–17.

Jucker, Andreas H. (2018). Apologies in the history of English: Evidence from the Corpus of Historical American English (COHA). *Corpus Pragmatics* 2 (4), 375–98.

Jucker, Andreas H. (2020). *Politeness in the History of English. From the Middle Ages to the present day*. Cambridge: Cambridge University Press.

Jucker, Andreas H. & Kopaczyk, Joanna. (2017). Historical (Im)politeness. In Culpeper, Jonathan, Haugh, Michael & Kádár, Dániel Z., eds., *The Palgrave Handbook of Linguistic (Im)politeness*. London: Palgrave Macmillan, pp. 433–59.

Jucker, Andreas H. & Taavitsainen, Irma. (2008). Apologies in the history of English. Routinized and lexicalized expressions of responsibility and regret. In Jucker, Andreas H. & Taavitsainen, Irma, eds., *Speech Acts in the History of English* (Pragmatics and Beyond New Series 176). Amsterdam: John Benjamins, pp. 229–44.

Jucker, Andreas H. & Taavitsainen, Irma. (2014). Complimenting in the history of American English: A metacommunicative expression analysis. In Taavitsainen, Irma, Jucker, Andreas H. & Tuominen, Jukka, eds., *Diachronic Corpus Pragmatics* (Pragmatics & Beyond New Series 243). Amsterdam: John Benjamins, pp. 257–76.

Jucker, Andreas H., Schneider, Gerold, Taavitsainen, Irma & Breustedt, Barb. (2008). Fishing for compliments: Precision and recall in corpus-linguistic compliment research. In Jucker, Andreas H. & Taavitsainen, Irma, eds., *Speech Acts in the History of English* (Pragmatics & Beyond New Series 176). Amsterdam: John Benjamins, 273–94.

Jucker, Andreas H., Schneider, Klaus P. & Bublitz, Wolfram, eds. (2018). *Methods in Pragmatics* (Handbooks of Pragmatics 10). Berlin: De Gruyter Mouton.

Jucker, Andreas H., Schreier, Daniel & Hundt, Marianne, eds. (2009). *Corpora: Pragmatics and Discourse. Papers from the 29th International Conference on English Language Research on Computerized Corpora (ICAME 29)*. Ascona, Switzerland, 14–18 May 2008. Amsterdam: Rodopi.

Kaindl, Klaus. (2013). Multimodality and translation. In Millán, Carmen & Bartrina, Francesca, eds., *The Routledge Handbook of Translation Studies*. London: Routledge, pp. 257–69.

Kärkkäinen, Elise. (2003). *Epistemic Stance in English Conversation. A Description of its Interactional Functions, with a Focus on* I think (Pragmatics & Beyond New Series 115). Amsterdam: John Benjamins.

Kim, Kyung H. (2014). Examining US news media discourses about North Korea: A corpus-based critical discourse analysis. *Discourse & Society* 25 (2), 221–44.

Kirk, John M. (2015). *Kind of* and *sort of*: Pragmatic discourse markers in the SPICE-Ireland Corpus. In Amador-Moreno, Carolina P., McCafferty, Kevin & Vaighan, Elaine, eds., *Pragmatic Markers in Irish English*, 89–113. Amsterdam: John Benjamins.

Koehn, Philipp. (2005). Europarl: A parallel corpus for statistical machine translation. In *Proceedings of Machine Translation Summit X: Papers*. Phuket, Thailand, pp. 79–86. https://aclanthology.org/volumes/2005 .mtsummit-papers/.

Koene, Ansgar & Adolphs, Svenja. (2015). Ethics considerations for corpus linguistic studies using internet resources. Working paper, HORIZON Digital Economy Research. http://casma.wp.horizon.ac.uk/wp-content/uploads/2015/ 04/CL2015-CorpusLinguisticsEthics_KoeneAdolphs.pdf.

Kohnen, Thomas. (1997). Toward a theoretical foundation of "text type" in diachronic corpora: Investigations with the Helsinki Corpus. In Hickey, Raymond & Kytö, Merja, eds., *Tracing the Trail of Time. Proceedings from the Second Diachronic Corpora Workshop. New College, University of Toronto, Toronto, May 1995*. Amsterdam: Rodopi, pp. 185–97.

Kohnen, Thomas. (2000). Corpora and speech acts: The study of performatives. In Mair, Christian, & Hundt, Marianne, eds., *Corpus Linguistics and Linguistic Theory. Papers from the Twentieth International Conference on English Language Research on Computerized Corpora (ICAME 20)*. Amsterdam: Rodopi, pp. 177–86.

Koteyko, Nelya, Nerlich, Brigitte, Crawford, Paul & Wright, Nick. (2008). "Not rocket science" or "no silver bullet"? Media and government discourses about MRSA and cleanliness. *Applied Linguistics* 29(2), 223–43.

Krendel, Alexandra, McGlashan, Mark & Koller, Veronika. (2022). The representation of gendered social actors across five manosphere communities on Reddit. *Corpora* 17(2), 291–321.

Kress, Gunther R. (2010). *Multimodality. A Social Semiotic Approach to Contemporary Communication*. London: Routledge.

Kress, Gunther R. & Van Leeuwen, Theo. (2001). *Multimodal Discourse: The Modes and Media of Contemporary Communication*. London: Arnold.

Krishnamurthy, Ramesh. (1996). Ethnic, racial and tribal: The language of racism? In Caldas-Coulthard, Carmen & Coulthard, Malcolm, eds., *Texts and Practices: Readings in Critical Discourse Analysis*. London: Routledge, pp. 129–49.

Landert, Daniela. (2014). *Personalisation in Mass Media Communication: British Online News between Public and Private* (Pragmatics & Beyond New Series 240). Amsterdam: John Benjamins.

Landert, Daniela. (2019). Function-to-form mapping in corpora: Historical corpus pragmatics and the study of stance expressions. In Suhr, Carla, Nevalainen, Terttu & Taavitsainen, Irma, eds., *From Data to Evidence in English Language Research* (Language and Computers 83). Leiden: Brill, pp. 169–90.

Leech, Geoffrey & Weisser, Martin. (2003). Generic speech act annotation for task-oriented dialogue. In Archer, Dawn, Rayson, Paul, Wilson, Andrew & McEnery, Tony, eds., *Proceedings of the Corpus Linguistics 2003 Conference* (Vol. 16). Lancaster: UCREL Technical Papers, pp. 441–6.

Locher, Miriam A. (2006). *Advice Online. Advice-Giving in an American Internet Health Column*. Amsterdam: John Benjamins.

Locher, Miriam A. (2020). Moments of relational work in English fan translations of Korean TV drama. *Journal of Pragmatics* 170, 139–55. https://doi .org/10.1016/j.pragma.2020.08.002.

Locher, Miriam A., & Graham, Sage L. (2010). Introduction to Interpersonal Pragmatics. In Locher, Miriam A. & Graham, Sage L., eds., *Interpersonal Pragmatics*. Berlin: Mouton, pp. 1–13.

Locher, Miriam A., & Messerli, Thomas C. (2020). Translating the other: Communal TV watching of Korean TV drama. *Journal of Pragmatics*, 170, 20–36. https://doi.org/10.1016/j.pragma.2020.07.002.

Locher, Miriam A., & Schnurr, Stephanie. (2017). (Im)politeness in health settings. In Culpeper, Jonathan, Haugh, Michael & Kádár, Dániel, eds., *Palgrave Handbook of Linguistic (Im)Politeness*. London: Palgrave, pp. 689–711.

Locher, Miriam A., & Thurnherr, Franziska. (2017). Typing yourself healthy: Introduction to the special issue on language and health online. *Linguistics Online*, 87(8/17), 3–24. http://dx.doi.org/10.13092/lo.87.4170.

Love, Robbie & Baker, Paul. (2015). The hate that dare not speak its name? *Journal of Language Aggression and Conflict*, 3(1), 57–86.

Lutzky, Ursula. (2012). *Discourse Markers in Early Modern English* (Pragmatics & Beyond New Series 227). Amsterdam: John Benjamins.

Lutzky, Ursula & Kehoe, Andrew. (2017a). "I apologise for my poor blogging": Searching for apologies in the Birmingham Blog Corpus. *Corpus Pragmatics* 1(1), 37–56.

Lutzky, Ursula & Kehoe, Andrew. (2017b). "Oops, I didn't mean to be so flippant": A corpus pragmatic analysis of apologies in blog data. *Journal of Pragmatics* 116, 27–36.

Lutzky, Ursula & Lawson, Robert. (2019). Gender politics and discourses of #mansplaining, #manspreading, and #manterruption on Twitter. *Social Media + Society* 5(3), 1–12. https://doi.org/10.1177/2056305119861807.

MacQueen, Kathleen M., Mclellan-Lemal, Eleanor, Bartholow, Kelly & Milstein, Bobby. (2008). Team-based codebook development: Structure, process, and agreement. In Guest, Greg & MacQueen, Kathleen M., eds., *Handbook for Team-Based Qualitative Research*. Lanham: ALTAMIRA, pp. 119–36.

Marchi, Anna & Taylor, Charlotte. (2009). Who was fighting and who/what was being fought? The construction of participants' identities in UK and US reporting of the Iraq War. In Garzone, Guiliana & Catenaccio, Paola, eds., *Identities across Media and Modes: Discursive Perspectives*. Bern: Peter Lang, pp. 259–87.

Matley, David. (2017). This is NOT a #humblebrag, this is just a #brag: The pragmatics of self-praise, hashtags and politeness in Instagram posts. *Discourse, Context & Media* 22, 30–8.

Maynard, Carson & Leicher, Sheryl. (2007). Pragmatic annotation of an academic spoken corpus for pedagogical purposes. In Fitzpatrick, Eileen, ed., *Corpus Linguistics beyond the Word: Corpus Research from Phrase to Discourse*. Amsterdam: Brill, pp. 107–15.

McEnery, Tony, Xiao, Richard & Tono, Yukio. (2005). *Corpus-Based Language Studies*. London: Routledge.

Méndez-Naya, Belén & Pahta, Päivi. (2010). Intensifiers in competition: The picture from early English medical writing. In Taavitsainen, Irma & Pahta, Päivi, eds., *Early Modern English Medical Texts: Corpus Description and Studies*. Amsterdam/Philadelphia: John Benjamins, pp. 191–213.

Messerli, Thomas C. (2020). Ocean's Eleven scene 12 – Lost in transcription. *Perspectives* 28(6), 837–50. https://doi.org/10.1080/0907676X.2019.1708421.

Messerli, Thomas C., & Locher, Miriam A. (2021). Humour support and emotive stance in comments on K-Drama. *Journal of Pragmatics* 178, 408–25. https://doi.org/10.1016/j.pragma.2021.03.001.

Miller, John, & Gergen, Kenneth J. (1998). Life on the line: The therapeutic potentials of computer-mediated conversation. *Journal of Marital and Family Therapy* 24(2), 189–202. https://doi.org/10.1111/j.1752-0606.1998.tb01075.x.

Morrow, Phillip R. (2012). Online advice in Japanese: Giving advice in an Internet discussion forum. In Limberg, Holger & Locher, Miriam A., eds., *Advice in Discourse*. Amsterdam: John Benjamins, pp. 255–79.

Norrick, Neal R. (2009). Interjections as pragmatic markers. *Journal of Pragmatics* 41(5), 866–91.

O'Keeffe, Anne. (2018). Corpus-based function-to-form approaches. In Jucker, Andreas H., Schneider, Klaus P. & Bublitz, Wolfram, eds., *Methods in Pragmatics* (Handbooks of Pragmatics 10). Berlin: De Gruyter Mouton, pp. 587–618.

O'Keeffe, Anne, Clancy, Brian & Adolphs, Svenja. (2020). *Introducing Pragmatics in Use*. 2nd ed. London: Routledge.

Palander-Collin, Minna. (1999). *Grammaticalization and Social Embedding. I THINK and METHINKS in Middle and Early Modern English*. Helsinki: Société Néophilologique.

Placencia, María Elena. (2012). Online peer-to-peer advice in Spanish Yahoo! Respuestas. In Limberg, Holger & Locher, Miriam A., eds., *Advice in Discourse*. Amsterdam: John Benjamins, pp. 281–305.

Proferes, Nicholas, Jones, Naiyan, Gilbert, Sarah, Fiesler, Casey & Zimmer, Michael. (2021). Studying Reddit: A systematic overview of disciplines, approaches, methods, and ethics. *Social Media + Society* 7(2), 1–14. https://doi.org/10.1177/20563051211019004.

Quo VaDis Project. (2022). Questioning vaccination discourse. www.lancaster.ac.uk/vaccination-discourse.

Ranganath, Rajesh, Jurafsky, Dan, & McFarland, Dan. (2009). It's not you, it's me: Detecting flirting and its misperception in speed-dates. In Koehn, Philipp & Mihalcea, Rada, eds., *Proceedings of the 2009 Conference on Empirical Methods in Natural Language Processing* (Vol. 1). Morristown, NJ: Association for Computational Linguistics, pp. 334–42.

Rebora, Simone, Boot, Peter, Pianzola, Federico, et al. (2021). Digital humanities and digital social reading. *Digital Scholarship in the Humanities* 36(S2), ii230–50. https://doi.org/10.1093/llc/fqab020.

Romero-Trillo, Jesús, ed. (2008). *Pragmatics and Corpus Linguistics: A Mutualistic Entente*. Berlin: Mouton de Gruyter.

Rudolf von Rohr, Marie-Thérèse. (2015). "You will be glad you hung onto this quit": Sharing information and giving support when stopping smoking online. In Smith, Catherine Arnott, & Keselman, Alla, eds., *Meeting Health Information Needs outside of Healthcare: Opportunities and Challenges.* Waltham, MA: Chandos/Elsevier, pp. 263–90.

Rudolf von Rohr, Marie-Thérèse. (2017). "If you start again, don't worry. You haven't failed": Relapse talk and motivation in online smoking cessation. *Linguistics Online* 87(8/17), 87–105. http://dx.doi.org/10.13092/lo.87.4174.

Rudolf von Rohr, Marie-Thérèse. (2018). Persuasion in smoking cessation online: An interpersonal pragmatic perspective. Freiburg i. Br.: Albrecht-Ludwigs-Universität Freiburg / Universitätsbibliothek Freiburg, https://freidok .uni-freiburg.de/fedora/objects/freidok:16755/datastreams/FILE1/content.

Rudolf von Rohr, Marie-Thérèse, & Locher, Miriam A. (2020). The interpersonal effects of complimenting others and self-praise in online health settings. In Placencia, Mária Elena & Eslami, Zohreh Rasekh, eds., *Complimenting Behavior and (Self-)Praise across Social Media.* Amsterdam: John Benjamins, pp.189–211.

Rudolf von Rohr, Marie-Thérèse, Thurnherr, Franziska & Locher, Miriam A. (2019). Linguistic expert creation in online health practices. In Bou-Franch, Patricia & Garcés-Conejos Blitvich, Pilar, eds., *Analysing Digital Discourse: New Insights and Future Directions.* London: Palgrave Macmillan, pp.219–50.

Rühlemann, Christopher. (2019). *Corpus Linguistics for Pragmatics: A Guide for Research.* Oxon: Routledge.

Rühlemann, Christopher & Aijmer, Karin. (2014). Corpus pragmatics: Laying the foundations. In Aijmer, Karin & Rühlemann, Christoph, eds., *Corpus Pragmatics: A Handbook.* Cambridge: Cambridge University Press, pp. 1–26.

Rühlemann, Christopher & Clancy, Brian. (2018). Corpus linguistics and pragmatics. In Ilie, Cornelia & Norrick, Neal R., eds., *Pragmatics and its Interfaces.* Amsterdam: John Benjamins, pp. 241–66.

Saldaña, Johnny. (2013). *The Coding Manual for Qualitative Researchers* (2nd ed.). London: SAGE Publications.

Simon-Vandenbergen, Anne-Marie. (2000). The functions of *I think* in political discourse. *International Journal of Applied Linguistics* 10(1), 41–63.

Soffritti, Marcello. (2018). Multimodal corpora in audiovisual translation studies. In Pérez-González, Luis, ed., *The Routledge Handbook of Audiovisual Translation* (1st ed.). London: Routledge, pp. 334–49.

Sotillo, Susana. (2012). Illocutionary acts and functional orientation of SMS texting in SMS social networks. In Ebeling, Signe Oksefjell, Ebeling, Jarle & Hasselgård, Hilde, eds., *Aspects of Corpus Linguistics: Compilation, Annotation, Analysis* (article 10). Helsinki: VARIENG, https://varieng.helsinki.fi/series/volumes/12/index.html.

Suhr, Carla & Taavitsainen, Irma, eds. (2012). *Developing Corpus Methodology for Historical Pragmatics* (Studies in Variation, Contacts and Change in English 11). Helsinki: VARIENG. https://varieng.helsinki.fi/series/volumes/11/.

Taavitsainen, Irma. (2001). Evidentiality and scientific thought-styles: English medical writing in Late Middle English and Early Modern English. In Gotti, Maurizio & Dossena, Marina, eds., *Modality in Specialized Texts*. Bern: Peter Lang, pp. 21–52.

Taavitsainen, Irma. (2002). Historical discourse analysis: Scientific language and changing thought-styles. In Fanego, Teresa, Méndez-Naya, Belén & Seoane, Elena, eds., *Sounds, Words, Texts and Change: Selected Papers from 11 ICEHL, Santiago de Compostela, 7-11 September 2000*. Amsterdam: John Benjamins, pp. 201–26.

Taavitsainen, Irma. (2009). The pragmatics of knowledge and meaning: Corpus linguistic approaches to changing thought-styles in early modern medical discourse. In Jucker, Andreas H., Schreier, Daniel & Hundt, Marianne, eds., *Corpora: Pragmatics and Discourse. Papers from the 29th International Conference on English Language Research on Computerized Corpora (ICAME 29). Ascona, Switzerland, 14-18 May 2008*. Amsterdam: Rodopi, pp. 37–62.

Taavitsainen, Irma. (2016). Genre dynamics in the history of English. In Kytö, Merja & Pahta, Päivi, eds., *The Cambridge Handbook of English Historical Linguistics*. Cambridge: Cambridge University Press, pp. 271–85.

Taavitsainen, Irma, Jucker, Andreas H. & Tuominen, Jukka, eds. (2014). *Diachronic Corpus Pragmatics* (Pragmatics & Beyond New Series 243). Amsterdam: John Benjamins.

Thurnherr, Franziska. (2017). "As it's our last exchange next time…". The closure initiation in email counseling. *Linguistics Online* 87(8), 213–36. http://dx.doi.org/10.13092/lo.87.4180.

Thurnherr, Franziska. (2022). *Relational Work and Identity Construction in Email Counseling*. Freiburg im Breisgau: Albrecht-Ludwigs-Universität Freiburg / Universitätsbibliothek Freiburg.

Thurnherr, Franziska, Rudolf von Rohr, Marie-Thérèse & Locher, Miriam A. (2016). The functions of narrative passages in three written online health contexts. *Open Linguistics* 2(1), 450–70. https://doi.org/10.1515/opli-2016-0024.

Tiedemann, Jörg. (2012). Parallel data, tools and interfaces in OPUS. In *Proceedings of the 8th International Conference on Language Resources and*

Evaluation (LREC'2012). www.lrec-conf.org/proceedings/lrec2012/pdf/463_
Paper.pdf.

Tognini-Bonelli, Elena. (2001). *Corpus Linguistics at Work*. Amsterdam: John
Benjamins.

Tonetti Tübben, Ilenia & Landert, Daniela. (2022). *Uh* and *um* as pragmatic
markers in dialogues: A contrastive perspective on the functions of planners
in fiction and conversation. *Contrastive Pragmatics* 1–32. https://doi.org/10
.1163/26660393-bja10049.

Tottie, Gunnel. (2011). *Uh* and *um* as sociolinguistic markers in British English.
International Journal of Corpus Linguistics 16(2), 173–97.

Tottie, Gunnel. (2014). On the use of *uh* and *um* in American English. *Functions
of Language* 21(1), 6–29.

Tottie, Gunnel. (2019). From pause to word: *Uh, um* and *er* in written American
English. *English Language and Linguistics* 23(1), 105–30.

Traugott, Elizabeth Closs. (2015). "Ah, pox o' your pad-lock": Interjections in
the Old Bailey Corpus 1720–1913. *Journal of Pragmatics* 86, 68–73.

Tyrkkö, Jukka, Hickey, Raymond & Marttila, Ville. (2010). Exploring Early
Modern English medical texts. Manual for EMEMT Presenter. In
Taavitsainen, Irma & Pahta, Päivi, eds., *Early Modern English Medical
Texts: Corpus Description and Studies*. Amsterdam: John Benjamins, pp.
219–77.

Vaughan, Elaine, McCarthy, Michael & Clancy, Brian. (2017). Vague category
markers as turn-final items in Irish English. *World Englishes* 36(2), 208–23.

Virtanen, Tuija & Halmari, Helena, eds. (2005). *Persuasion across Genres*.
Amsterdam: John Benjamins.

Weisser, Martin. (2010). Annotating dialogue corpora semi-automatically:
A corpus-linguistic approach to pragmatics. Habilitation (professorial) the-
sis, University of Bayreuth.

Weisser, Martin. (2014). Manual for the Dialogue Annotation & Research Tool
(DART). http://martinweisser.org/publications/DART_manual.pdf.

Weisser, Martin. (2015). Speech act annotation. In Aijmer, Karin &
Rühlemann, Christopher, eds., *Corpus Pragmatics: A Handbook*. Cambridge:
Cambridge University Press, pp. 84–114.

Weisser, Martin. (2018). *How to Do Corpus Pragmatics on Pragmatically
Annotated Data: Speech Acts and Beyond*. Amsterdam: John Benjamins.

Whitt, Richard J. (2016). Using corpora to track changing thought styles:
Evidentiality, epistemology, and Early Modern English and German scientific discourse. *Kalbotyra* 69, 265–91.

Zufferey, Sandrine & Cartoni, Bruno. (2014). A multifactorial analysis of
explicitation in translation. *Target* 26(3), 361–84.

Acknowledgements

Daniela's work on this Element was conducted at the University of Basel as well as at Heidelberg University. Miriam wishes to thank the University of Basel for financing a research leave in spring 2022 and Korea University in Seoul for hosting her during the writing period of this book. We thank the anonymous reviewers and general editors for their constructive feedback, which helped to strengthen our line of argumentation. This open access manuscript has been published with the support of the Swiss National Science Foundation.

Funding Statement

Published with the support of the Swiss National Science Foundation.

Cambridge Elements ≡

Pragmatics

Jonathan Culpeper
Lancaster University, UK

Jonathan Culpeper is Professor of English Language and Linguistics in the Department of Linguistics and English Language at Lancaster University, UK. A former co-editor-in-chief of the *Journal of Pragmatics* (2009–14), with research spanning multiple areas within pragmatics, his major publications include: *Impoliteness: Using Language to Cause Offence* (2011, CUP) and *Pragmatics and the English Language* (2014, Palgrave; with Michael Haugh).

Michael Haugh
University of Queensland, Australia

Michael Haugh is Professor of Linguistics and Applied Linguistics in the School of Languages and Cultures at the University of Queensland, Australia. A former co-editor-in-chief of the *Journal of Pragmatics* (2015–2020), with research spanning multiple areas within pragmatics, his major publications include: *Understanding Politeness* (2013, CUP; with Dániel Kádár), *Pragmatics and the English Language* (2014, Palgrave; with Jonathan Culpeper), and *Im/politeness Implicatures* (2015, Mouton de Gruyter).

Advisory Board
Anne Baron *Leuphana University of Lüneburg, Germany*
Betty Birner *Northern Illinois University, USA*
Lucien Brown *Monash University, Australia*
Billy Clark *Northumbria University, UK*
Chris Cummins *University of Edinburgh, UK*
Pilar Garcés-Conejos Blitvich *University of North Carolina at Charlotte, USA*
Andreas H. Jucker *University of Zurich, Switzerland*
Zohar Kampf *Hebrew University of Jerusalem, Israel*
Miriam A. Locher *University of Basel, Switzerland*
Yoshiko Matsumoto *Stanford University, USA*
Marina Terkourafi *Leiden University, The Netherlands*
Chaoqun Xie *Zhejiang International Studies University, China*

About the series
Cambridge Elements in Pragmatics showcases dynamic and high-quality original, concise and accessible scholarly works. Written for a broad pragmatics readership, it encourages dialogue across different perspectives on language use. It is a forum for cutting-edge work in pragmatics: consolidating theory, leading the development of new methods, and advancing innovative topics in the field.

Cambridge Elements $\equiv$

Pragmatics

Elements in the Series

Advice in Conversation
Nele Põldvere, Rachele De Felice and Carita Paradis

Positive Social Acts: The Brighter and Darker Sides of Sociability
Roni Danziger

Pragmatics in Translation: Mediality, Participation and Relational Work
Daria Dayter, Miriam A. Locher and Thomas C. Messerli

Fiction and Pragmatics
Miriam A. Locher, Andreas H. Jucker, Daniela Landert and Thomas C. Messerli

Corpus Pragmatics
Daniela Landert, Daria Dayter, Thomas C. Messerli and Miriam A. Locher

A full series listing is available at: www.cambridge.org/EIPR

Printed in the United States
by Baker & Taylor Publisher Services

Printed in the United States
by Baker & Taylor Publisher Services